The Unkindest Cut

The Emotional Maltreatment of Children

NAOMI HAINES GRIFFITH, M.A., M.S.W.
JANET S. ZIGLER, J.D.

RED CLAY & VINEGAR, LLP
NASHVILLE, TENNESSEE

The Unkindest Cut

The Emotional Maltreatment of Children

Naomi Haines Griffith, M.A., M.S.W.
and
Janet S. Zigler, J.D.

ISBN: 0-9723291-0-2

Library of Congress Control Number: 2002093777

Printed in the United States of America

Cover Illustration by Matthew Zigler

Red Clay & Vinegar, LLP
P. O. Box 68275
Nashville, Tennessee 37206
(888) 682-9090
redclaynhg@aol.com

The Unkindest Cut

Dedication

Although we can learn from seminars, books, and tapes, most of our parenting skills come from the "trial and error" or "on the job training" that begins on the day that our first child slips into the world.

Because we practiced on our own children, and now share the mistakes, humor, and delight of those experiences with anyone who will listen, we would like to dedicate this book to our children: Amelia and Wade Griffith, and Kirk and Matthew Zigler.

It is our hope that they understand the depth of our love for them.

Table of Contents

What Is the Unkindest Cut?

When Marc Antony eulogizes Julius Caesar in Shakespeare's account of Caesar's death, he refers to the betrayal by Brutus, Caesar's closest friend, as the "unkindest cut."

Antony is not referring to a physical cut from a sword, but to the emotional pain of disappointment that comes from being hurt by someone who is loved and trusted. The reader is led to believe that Caesar suffered most from the pain of this betrayal rather than from the cut of the sword.

The wounds of emotional maltreatment of children, inflicted by the hands of people they love, is similarly "the unkindest cut."

We must come to a common understanding of parental behaviors that are unacceptable and damaging and raise the public's awareness of the problem.

Introduction

Sticks and stones may break my bones, but words will never harm me"—the familiar playground philosophy we chanted as children—is simply untrue. We are now beginning to understand the impact of both emotional abuse and emotional neglect on the growth and healthy development of children. There is no doubt that, when children experience the invisible wounds of emotional maltreatment, they go out into the world with countless scars that impact their ability to live a normal, fulfilled life.

It is time for all of us to move one step forward in dealing with the relationships in families that damage children, children who will in short measure become the parents and guardians of our future. This new chapter in our journey to protect, nurture, and sustain children will bring resistance and new challenges, but it is vital in our quest for a world in which our children can experience a safe, nurturing environment.

Child welfare systems in this country are accustomed to investigating reports of physical and sexual abuse. This last stronghold of child abuse—emotional maltreatment—may be the most harmful of all the abuses that children suffer and may cause the longest-lasting damage. It will most likely be the most difficult to address because we like things to be concrete, provable, and obvious to the average person. This area of child maltreatment is none of these.

Like physical discipline, emotionally damaging words and actions often reflect cultural norms, family history and practice, and are generally regarded by the parent as acceptable. As a result, emotional abuse is often done in public with the parent feeling no apparent embarrassment or discomfort. A few months ago, an incident at a clinic bore this assertion out. Sitting in a doctor's waiting area, two young boys, probably eight and six years old, were playing in an alcove set up for children with toys, puzzles, and books. Suddenly, a man sitting across the room called out to one of the boys, "Get over here, Leroy." The older boy obviously knew the man was speaking to him and came over, looking apprehensive. The man, who could have been his father, grandfather, or perhaps his stepfather, harshly said, "Sit down!" and pointed to a low table in front of him. The boy sat directly in front of the man and waited. In a loud voice the man said, "Billy, you act like Leroy, so I'm going treat you like Leroy. Everybody knows what that means. That's who you are... Leroy." Billy began to cry.

It was obvious to anyone watching that Billy knew that he was being compared to someone totally undesirable, that he had been singled out and chastised in public, that everyone was looking, and that there was no caring in the adult's eyes. On the other hand, the man not only did not look embarrassed in front of the many patients who witnessed the incident, he actually looked satisfied. Either he believed, "I'll do what I want with the kid regardless of what you think," or he had no understanding of the hurt inflicted upon this child. Perhaps he was showing off or simply did not care about Billy's feelings.

The harm from this situation, whether intentional or not, was perpetrated by an adult who had no understanding of the emotional needs of the child, no capacity to provide emotional nurturance, and no grasp of the parent-child relationship.

This lack of understanding or awareness does not end with parents, but carries over into relationships children have with adults outside the home such as coaches, teachers, and extended family members. Each person in a child's life has a "realm of influence" depending on many factors such as time together, the level of esteem in which the child holds the person, the amount of power that the person has over the child, and the level of emotional involvement between the child and that person. The potential for harm extends to these relationships; therefore, our ability to educate and sensitize adults to the damage inflicted by emotional abuse must encompass the total community.

In the long process of addressing physical and sexual abuse over the last forty years, we have developed community standards about what the general public would accept relative to these behaviors. Certainly, there is no universal acceptance of one set of standards, but as a rule most people are aware of a basic general standard and know when the line has been crossed. This awareness of how the community feels does act as a deterrent for some adults.

It is time for all people concerned about children to address the fact that we are generally turning a blind eye to the existence of emotional maltreatment. It is time to do for emotional abuse what we have done for physical and sexual abuse. We must come to a common understanding of parental behaviors that are unacceptable and damaging and raise the public's awareness of the problem. Everyone has a part to play in this process.

This book is not a review of the technical literature and research relating to emotional maltreatment. Rather, it is a synthesis pulled together from thirty-five years of working in the field of strengthening families. We will take a look at a child's need to be emotionally nurtured in a safe and stable environment and examine the parental behaviors that interfere with that need. We will review the different statutory definitions of emotional maltreatment and neglect, and see how child protective agencies and the courts address these issues. Using this background material, our goal is to create a framework for discussion and reflection about the issue of emotional maltreatment. Once we have a basis for a common understanding we will urge communities as a whole to take action to give each child the chance to face life as an emotionally healthy person. Giving this gift to children will result in tremendous benefits to all.

Naomi Haines Griffith, M.A., M.S.W.
Janet S. Zigler, J.D.

Attention to the emotional maltreatment of children is the next step in our fifty year journey of defining the rights and needs of children.

Chapter One

The Challenge

As we begin our exploration of the issues surrounding emotional maltreatment, it is fascinating to look back from where we have come during the last half century with regard to our interventions on behalf of children. As a nation, we have a very strong bias against intervening in what goes on within a family. Nevertheless, we have slowly and progressively taken steps to protect what is generally termed "the best interests" of a child, recognizing that society does have an obligation to intervene on behalf of an otherwise defenseless young person. These steps have been taken despite strong opposition and criticism.

We first started by addressing the problem of the physical neglect of children in the '50's, determining that food, clothing, shelter, and medical care were required by a civilized culture. At the time of this early intervention, there were virtually no statutes to deal with child abuse. Some states had used their cruelty to animals laws in order to access the courts on behalf of children.

We next moved to physical abuse in the '60's, defining non-accidental injury and citing marks and bruises as evidence of unacceptable means of discipline. This concern was often met with resistance as some parents echoed the old refrain, "My daddy did this to me, and I turned out okay." However, states persisted in law and policy to set standards that separated physical abuse from discipline.

In the '70's, sexual abuse became our target as we attempted to expose and define it. It certainly was not a new phenomenon, but had existed in darkness, family secrets, and denial. Once it was brought into the open, the public was generally repulsed and outraged at violations of this taboo.

We are now facing what may be our greatest challenge—emotional abuse and neglect. Most people agree that physical and sexual abuse do not occur without the presence of emotional maltreatment. However, it is the carving out of emotional maltreatment as a distinct and separate form of child abuse that presents the problem. One can imagine a parent saying, "Well, you can tell me not to beat my child, but no one is going to interfere with what I can say to him." All professionals are aware of the outcry that could occur if we diligently address the subject of emotional maltreatment. However, attention to the emotional maltreatment of children is the next step in our fifty-year journey of defining the rights and needs of children.

The antithesis of a nurturing and stimulating environment within which a child will develop normally is emotional maltreatment. (We will use the term maltreatment to include both abusive and neglectful parenting behaviors.) However, the damage from this type of maltreatment is rarely the basis of interventions by agencies mandated to protect children, even though emotional abuse is part of reporting statutes in almost every state. In *Mental Health: A Report of the Surgeon General*, it was noted, "psychological maltreatment is believed to occur more frequently than physical maltreatment." (U.S. Department of Health and Human Services, 1999) Despite the prevalence of this type of abuse, there is no doubt that child protective services (CPS[1]) throughout the country do not generally deal with reports of emotional maltreatment. The parameters of concern about this situation were laid out in *A Report to Congress 1993: Study of High Risk Child Abuse and Neglect Groups* prepared by The National Center on Child Abuse and Neglect. The report included the following in its "Conclusions and Recommendations" section:

[1]Throughout this material, we will use the term "CPS" when referring to the state agencies that are charged with the investigation of child abuse and neglect.

> [A]ttention needs to be devoted to better defining CPS purview in connection with children who are emotionally maltreated. In the State Survey, children who are emotionally abused or neglected were identified as being potentially unserved or underserved, since these children are not always defined to be within the purview of the CPS agency. Moreover, even when emotional maltreatment is technically included within the agency's defined purview, it is typically not treated as a separate specified category. As a result, it may only be accorded attention when it occurs in conjunction with other maltreatment. Also, survey respondents reported that emotional maltreatment is generally more difficult to substantiate. Interestingly, victims of psychological maltreatment were also among the categories of children who were most often perceived as being in need of special CPS efforts without any such efforts reportedly having been made on their behalf. *Taken together, these facts converge on the implication that emotionally maltreated children are unserved or underserved by CPS relative to children who are maltreated in other ways.* These are the children most likely to "fall between the cracks" and/or to fall outside (or only ambiguously within) the CPS agency's purview. *Regrettably, they are also the children whose long-term developmental prospects bode least well in the absence of early intervention or treatment.* (U.S. Department of Health & Human Services, 1993) (emphasis added).

The fact that CPS generally does not address the issue of emotional maltreatment is not an indictment of the system. Rather it is symptomatic of the fact that society as a whole does not place a great priority on or have a great deal of understanding about the devastating impact of this type of abuse. This lack of attention needs to change and perhaps is beginning to change because we, at last, are seeing research that confirms how destructive such maltreatment is to a child, and the great cost to society of ignoring this destruction.

Recent developments in the field of brain research have brought home to thoughtful professionals an understanding of the toll that emotional abuse and neglect takes on the development of children. Whereas once there was only anecdotal psychological and behavioral evidence of the impact of abuse on a child's growth and development, brain research has now confirmed the physiological impact of abuse on the development of the brain of a child, particularly birth to age three. There is now overwhelming evidence that a child's environment will determine how a child views and reacts to the world. "It is now clear that what a child experiences in the first few years of life largely determines how his brain will develop and how he will interact with the world throughout his life." (Ounce of Prevention Fund, 1996)

There is now overwhelming evidence that a child's environment will determine how a child views and reacts to the world.

As stated by noted pediatrician, T. Berry Brazelton: "Many of the most important personality traits, such as the capacities for relating to others, trust and intimacy, empathy, and creative and logical thinking, are largely determined by how we nurture a child's nature." (Brazelton & Greenspan, 2000)

The scientific explanations about how an infant's brain develops are fascinating, but certainly beyond the abilities of the authors to appropriately synthesize. Dr. Bruce Perry, formerly of Baylor College of Medicine and presently head of ChildTrauma Academy, does an excellent job of providing understandable explanations of the physiology of the developing brain as impacted by trauma, stress, violence, and neglect. For the purposes of our discussion, the core of the research supports findings that providing a nurturing, calm and safe atmosphere for a newborn will permit the growth and strengthening of the neural connections that allow the child to appropriately interact with his environment. This type of world allows the normal progression that leads to the development of language and the social and the adaptive skills necessary for a child to successfully deal with the stresses and strains of life.

In contrast, a child who is born into a world that is fearful, violent, traumatic and/or neglectful ends up developing and strengthening those neural pathways, which help him to survive in a hostile environment. "If a child lives in a threatening, chaotic world, his brain will be hyper-alert for danger; his survival may depend on it. But if this environment persists, and the child's brain is focused on developing and strengthening its strategies for survival, other strategies may not develop as fully. If a child lives in a world that ignores him, if he is not provided with appropriate stimulation for growth, his brain will focus on survival from day to day and may not fully develop healthy cogni tive and social skills." (Ounce of Prevention Fund, 1996)

Schools are particularly impacted by the harm done to children by emotional maltreatment.

Schools are particularly impacted by the harm done to children by emotional maltreatment. First, schools bear the brunt of dealing with children who come into the classroom unable to learn because of the chaotic and abusive environments in which they are being raised. The child whose brain develops in an environment where he is forced to live with the constant stress of learning to survive will arrive at school without the same tools for learning as a child who is being raised in a safe and nurturing world. As Perry points out:

> [T]eachers [observe] that many of the maltreated or traumatized children they work with are often judged to be bright but can't learn easily. Often these children are labeled as learning disabled. These difficulties with cognitive organization contribute to a more primitive, less mature style of problem solving - with aggression

> often being employed as a "tool." This principle is critically important in understanding why a traumatized child - in a persisting state of arousal - can sit in a classroom and not learn. The brain of this child has different parts of the brain "controlling" his functioning than a child that is calm. The capacity to internalize new verbal cognitive information depends upon having portions of the frontal and related cortical areas being activated. This, in turn, requires a state of attentive calm — a state the traumatized child rarely achieves. (Perry, 2001)

The education system, under federal mandates, has established a category of special education that targets children with emotional problems that hinder school performance. This category of special need is referred to by different labels in different states, e.g. emotionally conflicted, emotionally disturbed, and behaviorally disordered. All of these terms refer to a condition that is preventing the child from functioning effectively within the school setting, and federal guidelines mandate that specific steps must be taken by the school district in the attempt to meet the child's education needs.

The behaviors that set these children apart begin or encourage a process of alienation, which results in extreme anti-social behaviors. The child who is seen as aggressive, unfeeling, cruel, withdrawn, unable to assume responsibility for negative behaviors, consistently angry, the object or instigator of verbal putdowns, unable to understand his own feelings or the feelings of others, or consistently disliked by his peers should be the object of our attention and concern. This child lacks the emotional tools he or she will need to function safely and effectively in society. Education attempts to assist a child with diagnosed emotional problems to learn necessary coping skills such as how to get along with others in the classroom, decrease aggressive behaviors, verbally express anger and demonstrate conflict resolution. All of these skills are critical if a child is to be able to work within the classroom.

The second reason schools must be involved in understanding and evaluating the harm that exists because of emotional maltreatment is that, all too frequently, the school becomes the place where a child finally acts out his anger. The child who experiences emotional abuse may not show the results immediately. He may be very quiet at school, and our expectations of behavior for children say that if a child is quiet, then everything is all right.

The quiet child, as a result of abuse, may strike out years later at everyone in the class, and no one knows why.

Perry states: "Organizing childhood experiences can be consistent, nurturing, structured, and enriched, resulting in flexible, responsible, empathic, and creative adults. Conversely, neglect, chaos, violence, and threats create impulsive, aggressive, remorseless and anti-social individuals." (Perry, 1998a) The quiet child, as a result of abuse, may strike out years later at everyone in the class, and no one knows why. All of a sudden, the child who was seen as "no problem" becomes a killer, and we begin to search for reasons. Waiting until there is an outcome of emotional maltreatment is not only irresponsible to the child, it can jeopardize the safety of those persons in the lives of these child victims.

In a review of the literature examining how maltreatment impacts brain development, the following conclusion was reached: "Maltreatment during infancy and early childhood has been shown to negatively affect early brain development and can have enduring repercussions into adolescence and adulthood.... [T]he experiences of infancy and early childhood literally provide the organizing framework for the expression of children's intelligence, emotions, and personalities. When those experiences are primarily negative, children may develop emotional, behavioral, and learning problems that persist throughout their lifetime, especially in the absence of targeted interventions." (National Center for Child Abuse and Neglect, 2001)

Children raised in an abusive environment face physical as well as mental and emotional problems. Kessler and Dawson point out in their extensive work on failure to thrive and pediatric malnutrition that, although we do not have enough research to make a definitive statement about the relationship of child abuse to serious health problems, child abuse may be associated with inadequate growth, citing a study where 26% of a research group of abused children experienced growth impairment. (Kessler & Dawson, 1999)

Children raised in an abusive environment face physical as well as mental and emotional problems.

In addition to the research that helps us understand the devastating impact of abuse and neglect upon children, there also is research that has focused upon those things in the life of a child that have a positive impact. In 1997, the first results from a research project conducted by the Adolescent Program, University of Minnesota, and the Carolina Population Center, University of North Carolina Chapel Hill, were presented in the *Journal of the American Medical Association.* The authors identified the following objective of the study: "To identify particular risk and protective factors at the school, family, and individual levels as they relate to four broad domains critical of adolescent health and morbidity (emotional health, violence, substance abuse, and sexuality)...." (Resnick, Bearman, Blum et al., 1997). In lay terms, the focus of the study was to determine what helps to keep our young people alive and away from self-destructive behaviors. What goes right in the lives of young people and protects them from getting involved in situations that could cause permanent harm?

The authors state, "Specifically, we find consistent evidence that perceived caring and connectedness to others is important in understanding the health of young people today." In this extensive longitudinal study, protective factors are identified that impact the safety of adolescents where drugs, alcohol, suicide, violence, and other destructive behaviors are concerned. The authors observed notable consistency across the domains of risk where the role of parents and family in shaping health of adolescents is evident. The first protective factor that greatly influences risky behaviors in adolescents is the presence or absence of connected, caring parents. The authors point out the simple presence of a parent in the home is helpful, but the presence is "less significant than parental connectedness (e.g., feelings of warmth, love, and caring from parents)." With this in mind, we must look at healthy family functioning as a public health issue, not just a sociological one. Relationships within a family directly affect whether a child engages in self-destructive behaviors that may result in death or injury to others.

The first protective factor that greatly influences risky behaviors in adolescents is the presence or absence of connected, caring parents.

A second protective factor in the life of an adolescent concerns the child's school. Although high expectations were a part of the protective factor, more important protections involved a child's feeling close to people at school, feeling like a part of the school, and feeling that teachers treated children fairly. There was a consistent finding that students who were well connected to their schools consistently engaged in less risky activities.

This preliminary result regarding schools has been followed up with additional analysis of the data gathered by the longitudinal study. In *Promoting School Connectedness: Evidence from the National Longitudinal Study of Adolescent Health*, the authors found that "when adolescents feel cared for by people at their school and feel like a part of their school, they are less likely to use substances, engage in violence, or initiate sexual activity at an early age" (McNeely, Nonnemaker, Blum, 2002). Specifically, it was noted:

> school connectedness is maximized when the social environment meets [students'] core developmental needs. The main developmental needs of middle and high school students include steadily increasing opportunities for autonomy, opportunities to demonstrate competence, caring and support from adults, developmentally appropriate supervision, and acceptance by peers.

In discussing the results of their analysis, the authors state that school connectedness improves where classrooms are well managed by the teachers: "When teachers are empathetic, consistent, encourage student self-management, and allow students to make decisions, the classroom management climate improves."

These research findings link the health and/or survival of the child with an emotional connection to one or more caring, empathic adults. This provides the justification for making emotional health, or the absence thereof, e.g. emotional maltreatment, a factor in determining whether a child is in imminent harm from abuse. This research examines these destructive behaviors in a context of health and survival, making emotional health a standard for safety and/or survival.

These new pieces of research help us frame the challenge facing us as we confront the need to move aggressively forward in attacking emotional abuse and neglect. A child raised in the absence of caring, empathetic adults faces a lifetime of struggle with the psychological and social deficits inflicted by those responsible for his care. That child will have difficulty doing well in school, working well with others in a job setting and

A child raised in the absence of caring, empathetic adults faces a lifetime of struggle with the psychological and social deficits inflicted by those responsible for his care.

creating a healthy family unit of his own. On the other hand, a child born into a loving, stable, and safe environment will be given an opportunity for reaching his potential and for avoiding destructive behaviors that could put his life at peril.

The potential cost to society for failing to become proactive when so much is at stake for children is enormous. All of those involved with children need to take stock as to where they presently stand in understanding both the healthy and the unhealthy aspects of the emotional life of a child.

The next portions of this book are aimed at providing a basis for a common understanding of what constitutes emotional health, what emotional maltreatment looks like and how institutions (legislatures, CPS, and the courts) are presently dealing with the problem. From there, we will suggest ways for each and every person concerned with the "best interests" of children to help meet the challenge of protecting children from emotional abuse and neglect.

Empathy lends an atmosphere of safety to a child's life where energy does not have to be spent on survival, wariness, and caution.

Chapter Two

Developing Emotional Health in Children

What do we mean when we talk about a child being emotionally healthy? We are talking about skills and behaviors that are necessary for children to be successful in life—first in school and later at home and in the workplace. These skills and behaviors involve an ability to form and sustain friendships and relationships. Such skills include problem solving, conflict resolution, leadership, self-control, and resilience in the face of difficulties. Behaviors such as an ability to show friendliness and kindness, and to get along with and be respectful of the feelings of others are all a part of a child who is emotionally healthy. Children (and adults) who have these qualities will be well liked and others will want them to be a part of their lives. Such children will not be ostracized from the group and will not become the focus of ridicule and scorn.

Emotional health became a topic of much interest and discussion with the publication of Daniel Goleman's books, *Emotional Intelligence* in 1995 and *Working with Emotional Intelligence* in 1998. Although certainly not the first psychologist to deal with the subject, Goleman's well-written books pulled together research demonstrating that the success of a child frequently depended not upon his IQ, but rather on how well he was able to interact emotionally and socially with his environment. Indeed, Goleman pointed out studies confirming that a person with a lesser IQ who has good "emotional intelligence" generally will do better in the workplace and in life as a whole than a person with a high IQ who has a limited ability to interact appropriately with others.

In a family that is healthy and nurturing, each family member has an empathetic relationship with other family members as well as people outside the family.

Those writing on the subject of emotional health and intelligence agree that the critical element in nurturing these skills and behaviors is the presence of parenting that is empathetic. Empathy is our ability to feel what another person feels. It is the ability to step outside ourselves and see another's position or perspective. It is our ability to feel the pain, joy, hurt, and happiness of another. It is the part of us that makes us human, caring, and truly loving. Empathy is the antithesis of selfishness or self-centeredness. It is the bridge between two persons over which a healthy emotional connection is made.

In a family that is healthy and nurturing, each family member has an empathetic relationship with other family members as well as people outside the family. This quality is the basis for trust, respect, and support, for it allows one person to feel for someone other than himself or herself. Such parenting encourages empathy in a child. It allows a child to feel for others, get outside himself and see another's perspective, recognize, and understand his own feelings, as well as recognize correctly the range of feelings and emotions in others.

This quality of empathy is developed early in life, especially in the first five years. (Goleman 1995) According to Goleman, these first five years are crucial; after that time, it is more difficult to cultivate empathy. As empathy is shown consistently to a young child, the child responds, and learns this as an appropriate response to others. In these relationships empathy is shown to the child through words, facial expressions, body language, and attitude.

In children, the presence of empathy allows a child to not only learn and absorb the quality of empathy, it gives the child the environment where he or she can relax, be unafraid, and confidently know that someone truly cares and will be there. This is a child whose normal developmental process of learning can proceed unhindered. Empathy lends an atmosphere of safety to a child's life where energy does not have to be spent on survival, wariness, and caution.

Beyond the basic requirement of empathy, Goleman identifies seven components for what he terms "emotional intelligence" or what others may call emotional health in children. His findings suggest that these characteristics in children are excellent indicators of success in school as well as vocationally.

Confidence

This is where a child feels that he or she has control or mastery over a part of his life, a set of skills, or an activity. Here the child gains positive feelings about himself from knowing that he is able to do something well. This ability does not have to be based on a traditional talent or skill, but just an expertise or accomplishment that the child feels is important. Adults often see one skill as much more important than others and, if the child cannot excel in that area, he may feel defeated. These areas are ones that the adult values, not necessarily those where the child has an aptitude or even interest. Playing the piano, making the soccer team, or competing in an activity such as Odyssey of the Mind may be too large for a child to address. A sense of confidence may come from a much smaller accomplishment such as drawing a good cartoon, participating in the church choir, or helping teach young children in summer activities.

A sense of competence seems to give us backbone or courage about our interaction and place in the world. In addition, this feeling of control or mastery definitely allows us to see at least some things as predictable in the world where most things are not within our control.

This feeling of confidence naturally adds to our sense of worth and value. A child who can say to himself or others, "I worked with the Boys and Girls Club™ T-Ball program this year, and our team was runner-up in the league," can take pride in his or her part in this accomplishment. There is no need to be the starting pitcher on the varsity team in order to gain confidence.

Curiosity

This element of emotional intelligence involves the propensity for risk. A child needs to believe that he can reach out beyond the comfortable or known, and the result can be good and positive for him. This curiosity, coupled with confidence, becomes a blueprint for school success as well as vocational success. This element is fostered by a voice in his life that says, "Go on and try it. Nothing ventured, nothing gained. If it works out, then great, and if it doesn't, try something else." A child needs to feel permission to try, regardless of the outcome.

To be able to reach out and try something new, a child needs a secure foundation to which he can return for reassurance. A young child might readily explore a new playground, but wants to check occasionally to insure that the parent is close by. A wave of a hand or a quick hug verifies that everything is fine. This security lays the child's foundation for exploring and interacting with something unfamiliar. Knowing a solid underpinning exists in life allows a child to explore his or her world with confidence.

Too often parents want to protect or shield their children by shaping risk to try and ensure success. However, the testing of the child, even with risk, has value if the climate is positive and supportive. It does not matter if the outcome is not what the child wanted or expected. Failure in this sense is a fear of even trying. We all learn from situations that are both positive and negative in outcome. On the other hand, the parent may have an unfulfilled personal goal that he wants to vicariously achieve through the child. This need translates into great pressure for the child who may not be able to satisfy the parent's goal.

Curiosity is a personal feeling of approval a child needs in order to move forward, take selected risk, and follow interests. It is this self-permission that spawns the entrepreneur, the visionary, and the creative mind.

Self-Control

This element is referred to by Goleman as "a sense of inner control" that is developed over time, allowing the child to see the consequences of his behavior and set limits on himself. With encouragement from adults in his life, the child learns to look carefully at what is or is not in his best interest. The development of an internal process of evaluation becomes the basis for this inner voice.

As children are socialized, they meet with consequences for all behaviors.

As children are socialized, they meet with consequences for all behaviors. A consequence can be positive or negative as determined by the environment. Touching a hot stove will bring a negative consequence. Staying in the yard as directed should bring a positive consequence. With repetition and reinforcement, the child internalizes the value of the experience, and after a while, he or she will react almost automatically without having external prompting. This becomes the inner voice.

Unfortunately, this inner voice is not a part of the new baby package. Babies come here wanting "what they want when they want it." The development of the inner voice is a process over time where children are able to personally see, with repetition, that what they thought they wanted may not be in their best interest. The ability to think through consequences and to control impulsive behavior has been demonstrated to be a valid predictor of success in school and of increased SAT scores. (Goleman, 1995)

Most adults do not have to go through a litany of questions regarding the wisdom of driving under the influence of alcohol. Over the years, fear of an accident, hurting someone, or getting a citation turn into a routine that does not require much thought. However, to a sixteen year old, this may not be so ingrained, and the inner voice may be small or non-existent. However, if that same child has experienced an inner voice in the past in regard to other issues, then he is more able to transfer this approach to driving under the influence. This child is much more likely to ask himself, "Is this in my best interest?"

Intentionality

The child who is emotionally healthy feels that his life has an impact on the world around him. This element is closely tied to what is generally referred to as self-esteem, for each of us needs to feel that our life, our existence, is important and significant to others.

The impact that the child decides to make upon the world can be positive or negative. Many opportunities exist for children to feel that impact. It can easily translate into a negative impact where a child feels importance through such activities as gangs, bullying, speeding, or other self-destructive behaviors. The child makes the impact, but it is not one that enhances the child's life.

Since the impact that most of us seek to promote is positive, it is never too early to provide opportunities in a child's life where he can see he has made a beneficial, valued impact on the family, the community, or in the lives of friends. It is important that this impact is acknowledged and confirmed for children until they are able to do this for themselves.

The positive opportunities are not always alluring or easy to access and often must be provided and nurtured by adults in the child's life. Volunteering in Special Olympics, mentoring a non-reading child, visiting in the nursing home, or other such activities are usually encouraged by adults and defined by groups such as church, Scouts, or school organizations. However, it has more impact and significance if the family engages in a volunteer activity together. Then the act is reinforced by the participation and approval of the parents or other family members.

Relatedness

The child is able to engage others and be understood. Here the child with "emotional intelligence" is able to talk with adults as well as peers and feels that those persons understand what he is saying, even if they do not agree. This gives the child an opportunity to share dialogue with adults and accomplishes several positive outcomes. In the first place, the child feels the adult is accessible and interested. This dialogue, initiated by the child, satisfies the need to "get on the record" with opinions with someone who is willing to truly listen, providing a framework or groundwork for future discussions about more complex issues that may be initiated by the adult.

Wrong ideas that aren't shared can translate into destructive behaviors and can cause hurt.

Secondly, this engagement allows the adult to get a glimpse of where this child stands, how he is thinking, and to evaluate the need for any further discussion. Even when the child follows a flawed line of reasoning, the sharing of this is valuable to the adult, for it may offer insights into behaviors or other problems. Wrong ideas don't hurt. Wrong ideas that aren't shared can translate into destructive behaviors and can cause hurt.

Finally, engaging others is critical for overall success—and a child needs the practice, whether the adult happens to agree with him or not. Throughout our lives, we must be able to speak up, state our position or even go against the prevailing opinion. Providing children with safe opportunities to do this will allow them to refine the skill of constructive dialogue.

Capacity to Communicate

The child is able to share ideas and feelings with others. Since most communication with children involves directions or instructions, very little conversation between adults and children involves anything except the sharing of data. It takes knowledge, skill, and practice to be able to go beyond stating a tangible fact and moving to an intangible idea or feeling.

First, the child must be able to identify and name his own feelings. Words such as *confused, hurt, afraid,* or *disappointed* and their meanings must be taught, and there are many others with subtle shades of meaning. This process, begun early in a child's life, becomes important to his understanding of self and others. The vocabulary of feelings is unlike any other, for each feeling must be felt, identified, and learned.

This process of learning also includes the ability to recognize and name the feelings of others accurately. Consequently, the child is able to interpret, understand, and relate to the feelings of others, enhancing his ability to be empathetic.

Finally, capacity to communicate includes the ability to articulate and share an idea. This moves the child from a one dimensional being to a person who interacts and appreciates the world on many levels. Knowing the capitals of the fifty states or the formula for finding the area of various shapes may be important to some since it is absolute, but learning to share an idea or thought of our own takes us to a very different place in relating to others.

The child who has emotional intelligence is able to balance his or her needs with the needs of others.

Cooperativeness

The child who has emotional intelligence is able to balance his or her needs with the needs of others. This balancing requires that several pieces be put together. The child must be able to assess his own feelings and needs correctly. Next, there must be an assessment of the feelings and needs of others. Finally, there must be a process that results in an outcome equitable to both.

The culmination of these skills as well as a great deal of self-reflection and insight is the final step in the journey to emotional intelligence. Here we achieve the balance that is vital to job satisfaction, healthy family relationships, and an overall sense of purpose for our lives. We are able to see ourselves as a piece, albeit an important piece, in the greater process of life. The child who is able to see early that he is working in and among others who have opinions, feelings, and needs becomes the adult who demonstrates empathy, who is a valued team member, who attracts positive, caring people, and who understands his value to the world.

Certainly this element most dramatically reflects the child's ability to empathize with others in his world, feeling what they feel, and adjusting his behavior accordingly to respect their needs and feelings. It would bother him to do otherwise.

• • • • • •

It is interesting to note that several of these emotional intelligence elements are the same as those identified as those that result in positive school connectedness. (McNeely, Nonnemaker, Blum, 2002) That study found that giving students opportunities to "demonstrate competence" and provide appropriate opportunities for decision making and "self-management" promoted the protective factor of a school able to reduce the risk of destructive behaviors in their students. Once again, the point needs to be made that schools that focus on assisting students to be emotional healthy will reap the benefits of better test scores and less violence.

The elements of emotional intelligence that Goleman identifies as critical for emotional health as well as for success, are cultivated and encouraged by adults in a child's life through appropriate modeling, instruction, and explanation. Attitudes and behaviors in the home that support the development of these elements in the child are positive and desirable. Conversely, the behaviors that hinder or impede the development of these elements must be regarded as emotionally abusive or neglectful.

The first function of family is to protect the child, providing a secure environment where the child may grow and develop. The family is society's first defense for children.

Chapter Three

Developing Emotionally Healthy Children

What do children need to be emotionally healthy? What is a healthy adult-child relationship? How do we foster the elements of emotional intelligence in children? We have traditionally attempted to isolate negatives and impairments. However, we think it makes more sense to identify commonalities that are found in families where children, for the most part, thrive and become contributing citizens. This does not mean that the children of these families sail through life without adversity, setbacks or failures. It means that these children come out of childhood with a better sense of themselves and prepared to take their places in society. With this in mind, we will examine what appears to be good practice in the area of parenting. We will identify characteristics of families that we will categorize as healthy.

The first function of family is to protect the child, providing a secure environment where the child may grow and develop. The family is society's first defense for children. What do we want families to do to ensure the safety and emotional health of their children? What are some things that seem to make families function well? If it is possible to develop a consensus on general, healthy characteristics in families, then it is obviously much easier to identify those behaviors that hinder the development of emotional health in children.

All of these broad characteristics are certainly not found in any family, full-blown and complete. Rather these traits represent an evolving process of work and awareness where parents seek to demonstrate behaviors and activities that promote healthy interactions.

One young mother in Richmond, Virginia heard a presentation on building healthy families. She was able to identify characteristics that were, in some degree, in place in her family. During the next year she and her husband talked about the list and looked for ways to implement new behaviors. This mother felt this awareness and work had really paid off for her family, and both she and her husband had enjoyed addressing positive initiatives.

Most parents look at a list of desirable family characteristics and generally agree with them. They represent conventional wisdom, but young parents are too often looking for something flashy and new, rather than what has been proven over time. This assumption that new techniques are better discounts the value of basic common sense in parenting.

This assumption that new techniques are better discounts the value of basic common sense in parenting.

Another factor involved in the lack of proactive, positive parenting is laziness or apathy. As parents we let things go until they are broken or demand attention. Then we sit up, reach for a quick fix in a "how to" book, and lament the way families have deteriorated and changed. Of course families have changed, but what constitutes appropriate personal interaction has not, or should not, change. There are some constants in life, and they appear in healthy relationships, especially in the family.

With the frustration that can come from basic parenting, especially of adolescents, it is comfortable and easy for parents merely to give up, stating that they have lost their children to the "streets," friends or the influence of TV. This is contrary to the fact that parents are the greatest influence in a child's life, either proactively or by their resigning that role and allowing other influences to take over.

The discussion of negatives such as disrespect, violence, drugs, alcohol, and promiscuity make for a more dramatic dialogue than discussion of the development of an empathetic parent/child relationship. However, if we want a healthy family, we can't just throw up our hands at the negative influences in a child's life. Building a healthy family environment is cheaper, less painful and more effective. It is an approach that will not permit indifference or procrastination. Preventive health, in any form, is always active.

Therefore, we come to a strength-based approach to parenting. It is grounded in the idea that all families have similar needs and goals. This approach, unlike the old, deficit-based approach, does not single out some families as failures or impaired. Rather, it is predicated on the fact that all families have strengths on which they can build. Accepting that all family have strengths but need support and attention, the discussion begins with a look at the general characteristics or traits that are associated with healthy family functioning. Each of these elements is grounded on the existence of empathy between the parent and the child. The parent will model empathy to the child and will encourage the child to feel empathetic to others.

Trust

Families that approach emotionally healthy demonstrate a sense of trust among the family members. We use the word "trust" in many ways, but in this context, trust involves a set of understandings, all predicated on the presence of empathy. Trust means, "You will not knowingly hurt me."

This understanding or "given" in family relationships is the bedrock for other healthy relationship factors. This is not to say that a person will not be hurt by word or action of others, but it will not be intentional. Intent is the key factor in understanding the meaning of trust because it separates true abuse from an inadvertent mistake or breach of caring.

If a child knows that others in the family will not set out to hurt him, he can relax. There is no need to constantly be on guard or aware of danger. This understanding and trust lays a groundwork for the day-to-day rhythms of life that are not only healthy but allow children to use their energy to develop normally both emotionally and mentally. Energy does not need to be diverted from the normal developmental process.

The phrase naval officers use, “Stand down,” comes to mind here. It means that the need to be on alert or at battle stations does not exist, and the sailor can relax and resume normal duties. The presence of trust allows children to “stand down” and attend to the routines of life that are developmentally appropriate. There is no sense of constant danger; there is an atmosphere of safety.

Predictability

The element of trust in a family leads to a sense of predictability. Children who have experienced chaos and extreme family upheaval have said to me, “Lady, just tell me how it’s going to be. I think I can get used to it if you’ll tell me how it’s going to be.”

These statements from young children are strong reminders of our need to “know how it’s going to be.” We have long acknowledged the need for children to have resiliency, to be able to bounce back. This ability, however, is based on an understanding that the important things won’t change. Predictability is the heart of this understanding.

Children love routine, a rhythm that allows them to know what to expect. Again, this allows the child to avoid being preoccupied with worry or concern about situations that are normally associated with adult responsibilities. Getting up in the morning at a regular time, knowing there will be food to eat, seeing faces that show caring, knowing a parent will be there at 3:00 p.m. if she said she would, going to bed with a story or prayer and sleeping safely all are examples of these predictable rhythms of life that children need.

Children love routine, a rhythm that allows them to know what to expect.

Where a child lives, how much money is available, what the menu is or the education level of the parent have nothing to do with predictability. What does matter is that food will be shared equally, the parent will love regardless, and protection from harm is present. This trust factor reduces the stress and uncertainty and allows a child to expend energy where necessary—on developmental growth.

Being poor is not what is significant. What really matters is how the resources available to a family are used and shared. Many adults have said, "I grew up poor, with only beans and cornbread, and I really didn't know we were poor." Another statement from adults who seemingly function well is, "We didn't have much at all growing up, but it was okay." Those statements capture the idea of trust and predictability. No matter how little the family had, it was shared equally, and resources were not used to satisfy selfish desires of the parents for alcohol, drugs, or gambling. When a child sees that the parent takes what is available, regardless of how meager, and uses it well and fairly, the message is clear, "Mother and Daddy are doing the best they can."

This is one reason why poor parents can be good parents. They can be predictable in their love, attention, and responses. They can treat each child in a fair and equitable manner. These responses will outweigh the absence of expensive sneakers or ninety-six channels on the television. One of my most vivid memories of childhood is seeing my father take the glasses at supper and measure out the limited supply of milk equally among us. I may have wanted more, but I did not feel slighted or treated unfairly. There was no need to be resentful or bitter.

Predictability also involves the simple mandate, "Do what you say you will." Don't make casual promises, off-hand offers, or set dates and then simply ignore them. Being able to "count on" a parent's word is critical for a child's emotional health. Too often, adults throw out promises to look good at the moment, to placate, bribe, or manipulate a child, but feel no sense of responsibility to ensure that the promise happens. For that reason, a parent who waits to say, "We're taking a camping trip" immediately prior to leaving, is a thoughtful parent. Too many things can happen to change a plan, and the child doesn't care about or understand excuses.

A really tender spot involving predictability concerns pick-up times. If an adult says, "I'll be there to get you at 3:00," she should be there or be in the hospital. Children panic when they are left, thinking that perhaps no one will ever come to get them. To adults a twenty-minute delay is not much, but to a child it is an eternity. At the very least the adult should say, "I plan to be there by 3:00, but if the traffic backs up, it could be 3:10. Don't worry, I'm coming." If the past verifies the truth of this promise, then the child does not have to worry.

Respect

Respect is a word tossed about with many meanings. It has been trivialized to include a myriad of feelings. When parents say, "My children don't show me proper respect," what does that mean? Does it mean that the child did not say "sir" or "ma'am" or did not do as the parent directed? In peer usage one teenager says about another, "He disrespected me." He may also shorten the accusation to merely, "He dissed me." Whatever the adulteration of the word, there is an understanding that one person has not been treated as he feels he should be.

For many adults respect means looking up to, acquiescing, deferring, and listening to adults.

Older adults such as grandparents may remark, "Children today don't show respect to adults like we did growing up." Does that translate into, "Modern day children argue, offer opinions counter to the adult, disagree, and do not treat adults as special?" For many adults respect means looking up to, acquiescing, deferring, and listening to adults.

Whatever the use, there is one common, although inaccurate, understanding about the concept of respect. For most people, respect is something that is shown or demonstrated toward them as the receiver. The ordinary person thinks of respect as something they receive. We generally do not give as much though to how we demonstrate respect. This is especially true in regard to children.

> It is more appropriate to think of respect as a reciprocal interaction.

It is more appropriate to think of respect as a reciprocal interaction. It is a quality that is given and received equally. Respect is the value we accord to each other. For a family to function well, respect is given to all members just because they are human, live and breathe, and have being. Children and adults share respect equally.

There is a boutique in Birmingham, Alabama where the clothes are kept in the back of the store. A prospective customer goes in, tells the clerk what type of dress she needs and the size, and the clerk returns with one, draping it dramatically over her arms. Needless to say, the dresses are very expensive. Now, most of us will agree that we often take on the personality and characteristics of the people we serve. The general's aide speaks for the general. The doctor's receptionist speaks with authority and power, and of course, the salesperson takes on the personae of the regular customers. When we casually walk into that store looking scruffy and average, the clerk looks up and down as if to say, "You can't afford to buy here." She doesn't have to say a word to convey a lack of respect.

Each of us has been in a situation where we were not shown respect, and we felt it keenly. This lack of respect may have come from an employer, a public servant, a professional, or a co-worker. Regardless, it made us feel small, and it probably made us angry or resentful. It's an attitude that says, "You are not important."

Adults frequently equate respect with age, authority or power. We may also think respect means dominion. This erodes our ability to show respect to children. If we can move beyond this position and see respect as acknowledging essential value, then it will be easier to demonstrate mutual respect in a family. Respect is a "given" or understanding that we all have value just because we are human and deserve that distinction.

Nowhere is the showing of respect more important than in a family. All members must be important, and each one should be able to give and receive the confirmation that comes from knowing other family members value them. This valuing is not based on age, gender, IQ, talent or physical appearance. The value is inherent in every healthy relationship and becomes the foundation for mutual respect. Children are certainly not guaranteed any respect outside the home, especially from peers; therefore, the respect of the family becomes even more critical.

Respect involves listening, making eye contact, and asking the person's opinion.

Respect involves listening, making eye contact, and asking the person's opinion. It involves body language that is attentive and a tone of voice that is not impatient when time is being spent together. All of these intangibles of human interaction lead to respect, and the miracle is that when parents give it, they get it back.

Privacy

Each of us has a need to establish a personal realm, a sense of space for ourselves. It gives us a feeling of value and safety to "mark off" our territory. Certainly this is limited for a child, but, nevertheless, it is possible achieve in two significant areas.

Personal Property

Respect for private property is an element in the family that establishes guidelines of behavior that form the basis for healthy emotional interactions both inside and outside the home. Whether the property is a Picasso valued at millions or a set of Matchbox cars, the concept of private property is at stake.

Everyone in the family owns something, even if it is just the clothes on his or her back.

Respect for the person translates into a respect for the person's property. "This is mine, and this is yours" should be a litany heard regularly in the home as we teach young children this concept. The right to own property, according to English economist John Stuart Mill, is the difference between being civilized and not being civilized. It is not an idea that comes easily and is certainly not a value or understanding that is innate. It must be learned and we must teach it.

Buying a small hook and eye for a door to protect an older child's room and possessions from a younger child is a simple way of demonstrating this idea. Not allowing a child to ramble through a purse or billfold is another. Asking to "borrow" and seeking permission to use another's property also teaches the concept.

Teaching respect for personal property requires so much effort and repetition that most adults become lax with the lesson. Everything becomes a wash of "community property" until there is a crisis. The problem with this becomes apparent when the child goes to school. He takes the property of others, and this is not tolerated. Then he is regarded as a thief, all because the family could not teach, "This is mine, and this is yours."

Teaching respect for personal property requires so much effort and repetition that most adults become lax with the lesson.

Parents can help teach this concept by respecting the sanctity of a child's room. Knocking on the door or frame is a sign of respect, even if the door is open. Indiscriminate searching is not indicated without strong cause. If a parent thinks a child is harboring stolen property or selling drugs out of a stash in his room, a search could be justified. Random rifling of another person's property simply to satisfy our curiosity sends a message that will be translated into disrespect.

Body Privacy

Another important aspect of privacy involves the human body. In healthy families there is a respect and deference with regard to personal privacy. It makes us feel safe to bathe and change clothes in private. We like to attend to our personal needs by ourselves. Adults expect and treasure these rites of personal respect. As children grow and develop, they also need this personal privacy. It is given in steps as children learn to toilet alone, bathe alone and dress themselves. It is symbolic of our recognition of their maturity and responsibility. We need to talk about it, point it out and place value on these rituals.

In return, adults must demand the same respect. Children should not barge into adults' rooms or go into the bathroom unannounced. Most likely, they will sit outside the bathroom door, talk to us, color pictures for us to grade, and ask when we will be out. However, the line is established—even if total quiet is not.

The socialization process that involves respect for personal privacy teaches a child to respect his own body and the bodies of others.

Lack of respect for personal privacy or relaxing these lines of respect promote a familiarity among family members that hinders the development of socially acceptable behaviors in children. They do not need to go into the bathroom, even at daycare, without respecting the privacy of another child. The socialization process that involves respect for personal privacy teaches a child to respect his own body and the bodies of others.

There are various views about this subject that involve different cultures, philosophies, and mores. However, children must live in the world with others, and the subject of body privacy evokes responses in adults and other children that can stigmatize the child if his behavior is outside the realm of what is considered normal.

Parents often inquire about shared adult and child nudity in the home. Some parents feel this provides children with a more relaxed acceptance of their own bodies and their sexuality. Several questions come to mind. Even if the adults in the home are comfortable with nudity, does that mean that a child is also? What will happen as the child realizes that other families do not walk around naked? How does the child integrate this behavior at home and what is expected of him in other settings? In our society, common nudity between children and adults is not the norm, and it could be very difficult for a child to differentiate between family behaviors and those acceptable outside the home.

The point is obvious. The subject of privacy in regard to both property and the human body is important. Healthy families address this subject, talk about it and develop a routine approach that allows the child to relax and feel safe.

Children do not come into the world ready to work, to make a living, to have an ethic about dependability and steadiness that we treasure in adults.

Responsibility

The words *respond* or *response* reflect a person's interaction with his/her environment. From them comes the noun *responsibility*, which has a much more complex meaning. Responsibility carries a connotation of obligation, seriousness, and accountability. It implies that there is a societal norm for how one responds to the world, especially in the following two areas.

Learning to Work

Children do not come into the world ready to work, to make a living, to have an ethic about dependability and steadiness that we treasure in adults. These attitudes and skills are learned, and the learning begins very early. By the time a child enters kindergarten or first grade, many of the attitudes he or she needs to ensure success in the workplace are already present.

This begins with seeing adults work. Getting up in the morning, having a cup of coffee, and going out to work even when he doesn't want to go is surely one way a father says that work is important. A child who hears a mother say, "I'm not really feeling well today," and then sees her walk out the door soon gets the idea about responsibility.

My father drove almost two hours to be at work by 7:00 a.m., and my mother got up at 4 o'clock to spend that "getting ready" time with him. I could hear them in the kitchen in the early morning hours and feel the rush of cold winter air as he went out the front door to make a living for us. That object lesson that parents are supposed to provide for their children is irreplaceable for a child.

Another function of families that promotes health in children is the role that parents have in "teaching children how to work." This does not mean merely the assigning of tasks by the adult such as picking up toys, cleaning the room, or taking out the trash. It means training, which is a process that takes time and consistency. Responsibility is taught by working with the child, demonstrating the basic points of how a task is accomplished. This means explaining the desired outcome, assisting the child in the organization of the task into small parts, encouragement, and praise for accomplishment and success, even when it is small.

Responsibility is taught by working with the child, demonstrating the basic points of how a task is accomplished.

Let's take picking up toys as an example. Sending a young child to "pick up his toys" as the first step in training is ridiculous. Instead, start out with, "Let's pick up toys now," which involves participation by the adult. Dividing the task into parts, e.g. toy box pieces, shelf pieces, crayons in box, books on the bookshelf, allows the child to organize and not be overwhelmed with the big task. It also allows the adult to praise and encourage with each step. Later on, the child may be assigned the task alone. However, in most cases the adult must go and look at finished product, praise the good parts and discuss what needs to improve in order to get regular success.

This interaction is a perfect opportunity to discuss work, the dignity of work, and the respect that comes from work. Assignments for tasks in the home should reflect fairness and sensitivity to a child's abilities and age, and a conversation should explain the thought given to the decision. This "teaching how to work" is a very important process that must begin very early if we are to have a child who can go into a fast food restaurant as a teenager and be successful. By the time a child is sixteen, he or she needs to know about dependability, punctuality, teamwork, organization and self-motivation. The family provides the initial basis for this education process.

My mother felt it was her duty to teach me how to work. Early on, we'd work in the garden together, sticking beans and pinching worms off the cabbages. When I was in the seventh grade, she decided that I needed to learn how to work with her at the local department store. The first day that I reported to work with Mother, she was in the shoe department. She looked at me and said, "Now, Naomi, there are some things I want to tell you."

This was what you would call an "on the job" training session. The *first rule* she said was, "We don't jump tables here." Now, of course that didn't have any literal meaning. What she meant was, "We don't kill ourselves here." She said, "We don't jump tables, but we work steady."

That was the first rule, and she added later on like a postscript, "When you're not with a customer, you're supposed to be straightening." That meant that you were supposed to look busy whether you were busy or not. It was distracting to the customers and certainly to the manager to just stand around chewing gum and not doing anything. After customers came in, tore up the merchandise, got all of the boxes open, and all the shirts tumbled and out of side, straightening the store was very important. This was what we were supposed to be doing if we didn't have a customer.

"The *second rule*," she said, "is that everybody who comes in here is the same, and we treat them right." That laid the groundwork for the idea that there was no special treatment for customers—nobody got more or less regardless of how they looked or who they were. Mothers would bring babies with dirty diapers in for shoes, or they would come in with children who were dirty and eating bananas, and we would end up with banana peels all over the floor and candy wrappers stuck to the sizer. We just didn't notice it. I did what my mother always said, "You go on," and that means you just do your job with kindness.

The *third rule* that she talked about was, "Give the customer what they want. Don't argue with them. If they ask for size seven, give them a size seven even though you may know that they need a nine or a ten. People want to be in charge."

Later on she told me the *fourth rule*. "We don't make people buy anything." That was the understatement of the year. Mother was never pushy, just kind and friendly, always letting the customers look at the merchandise alone. She would be there if they needed help, but she did not try to push them into buying something. She had a real knack for sales.The customer would come in and say what she wanted or just say she was looking. If she said she was looking, Mother backed right off and went back to some little job. In the process of walking off she would say "Well, call me if you need me."

If the customer would say, "I'm looking for Sunday shoes, or a pair of white heels," Mother would show them what she had in their size. They would sit in the chair, and she would place the pair of shoes down beside them, saying, "You try them on and see if you need another size." She believed people like to try on their own shoes. She would go off and keep working. She did not sit there and watch every move they made. It took a lot of pressure off the customer. I watched this little way that she handled people; it was respectful but also very effective in sales.And so we started to work together. I really enjoyed working with Mother. More importantly, I learned so much about people, how to talk to them, and how to work with the other people in the store. Mother had truly taught me how to work.

Responsibility for One's Actions and Behaviors

The second aspect of responsibility involves our personal behavior with regard to others. The goal in a healthy family is for a child to be able to say, "I did this, I shouldn't have, and I'm sorry." Stepping up and taking responsibility for work not done, unkind words, disappointing others, and other actions that we deem unacceptable is critical to the development of empathetic, conscientious adults. Socicty despises excuses, blaming others, and a lack of caring about mistakes. This attitude of responsibility must be fostered in early childhood.

Adults demand that children do what they say they will in regard to curfews, chores and homework and impose punishments if they fail to carry through. Yet, all too often, we think it is all right for us to slide. It is interesting in our culture that when children forget or don't follow through, they are irresponsible. When older persons forget, they are senile. But when a parent drops the ball, they "just have too much on their minds." Children have a very keen sense of what is fair and unfair. Being held to a standard of responsibility not followed by the adults in the family will make a child resentful and angry. Our ability to be responsible and not make excuses will definitely set an example for children to develop these same standards.

The seeds of undesirable, sociopathic behavior that can flower in adulthood begin in early childhood when a child does not have to "face the music" for his or her behavior. An emotionally healthy outcome in families must begin with the responsible adults who model responsible behavior. This is not easy for us, because we hate to "lose face" to children. We have a part of us that says, "Adults don't apologize to children" yet this is required if we want to teach responsibility. We have to first step up and admit our errors.

Walking down that long hall to a child's room and saying, "I should not have said that to you. I lost my cool, and I'm sorry," is a courageous act on the part of an adult. It's difficult because we think that if we admit even a small flaw, we will lose our place of authority. Actually, the opposite is true. By accepting responsibility, we model accountability to our children and allow our children to see how we will try to remedy the problem. It builds strength and respect in the relationship, rather than compromising our position of leadership.

By accepting responsibility, we model accountability to our children and allow our children to see how we will try to remedy the problem.

There is also value in having a child see one parent or adult apologize to another. This places a stamp of approval on the act of admitting wrong and seeking forgiveness. Of course, there must be sincerity and kindness in these exchanges if the child is to see them as appropriate and loving. Our goal, after all, is to bring the child to a point where he will take responsibility for his own actions and behaviors.

Establishing Moral Baselines for the Family

Somewhere in the '60's most people stopped using the words "right" and "wrong" as if they were archaic or moralistic. We began to talk about "situational ethics" or see actions as if they were always "gray" instead of black or white. After thirty years of slipping around on moral issues, we need to get back to family discussions about what is acceptable or unacceptable in behaviors. We need a proactive approach where parents get on the record with their children about what their family stands for.

Some parents have lost their willingness to establish standards, perhaps fearing that if a child crosses the line they would not know how to react to or handle the situation. The fear of not being able to fully enforce a rule prevents some parents from taking a stand.

However, there is significant value in setting the standard. It makes a statement about what is right even if there is not full compliance.

Each family determines standards of behavior, and there is certainly no blueprint a family must follow. Each family should allow for differences in culture and custom. The family should sit down, discuss behaviors and come to a consensus on these standards. This process will bind the family into an understanding that could be called a "Family Code of Ethics" that is posted on the refrigerator. The fact that the whole family, parents as well as children, commits to the code builds a sense of trust and solidarity.

Families that are emotionally healthy establish this "Family Code of Ethics." It may not be written down, but there is an absolute understanding of expectations by all family members. Each family molds its own code of behavior based on parental expectations and behaviors, verbalization of what is expected from children and a consistent accountability. Everyone in the family is held to the same standard.

The process of creating a family code of right and wrong can be begun by asking parents, "Can you tell me five things that you could tell your children are wrong but are not against the law?" We are not talking about murder, rape, or robbery. These are wrongs that have been institutionalized by society. These five things are behaviors that in and of themselves will not land a child in prison, but will be unacceptable in your family. These behaviors have to do with how we treat each other day to day.

Although each family reaches its own consensus on ethics, some ideas for consideration include the following:

a. In our family we do not make fun of or ridicule people who have handicaps.

b. In our family we do not make racist, gender or ethnic jokes and comments.

c. In our family we do not take advantage of people to make ourselves look better.

d. In our family sarcasm and put downs are unacceptable.

e. In our family we do not have "name-calling."

Sometimes it is necessary to have long discussions to reach consensus on the ethics of family behavior, but all are held to the code once it is established.

Permission to Share Feelings

The home must be a safe place where we can let down, share our feelings with people who care and expect someone to listen with empathy. The world, be it school, the workplace, friends, or society, is often full of hurt, disappointment and anxiety. Each of us needs a place where we can reveal our true feelings without a fear of humiliation, rejection or embarrassment. That should be the very heart of a home.

In an emotionally healthy home, each family member can be vulnerable without having it used against him. Parents and children can share their hopes, dreams, and heartbreaks without a need to put up a front or risk emotional blackmail. Most children enter school each day, their loins girded, attempting to be brave, perfect, and stoic in order to present an image of strength. Adults show the same behaviors in the workplace or with their friends whose acceptance is sought and treasured. We are constantly on guard to say the right thing, wear the right clothes, hang with the right people and present a certain image.

A young child who comes home from school, walks in the door and says, "No one wants to play with me at recess cause I'm a nobody," is taking a chance when he shares. In so many ways, sharing our true feelings is being emotionally naked. We bare our hearts in hopes someone will care and seek to bind the wound. That is what an emotionally healthy home can do. Parents generally can't and shouldn't try to remedy the everyday problem. However, they must provide the safe haven of the family in order to give a child respite and emotional relief.

Asking a question such as, "How was school today?" will probably only get an answer such as "Okay" or "Fine." Instead, say "Tell me something good that happened at school today," or "Tell me something that hurt today" as a way to open the way for a more meaningful discussion. It is improbable that a child goes through a full day without a moment of hurt himself or for others. Questions such as these prompt the child to share feelings, and they also serve as an expression of interest on the part of the parent.

In addition to this aspect of safely sharing feelings, there is a second benefit. In the healthy family, the discussion that follows the emotional disclosure gives others in the family the opportunity to process with the child or adult what has happened, be a good sounding board, evaluate, and offer suggestions. It can become the forum for a child or adult to examine his thought processes, determine if he is reading the situation correctly, and make a plan for the future in dealing with the problem. In other words, the family is the first line of counseling, and it is in a safe, caring environment. Later, if more help is required, outside consultation is the logical step.

...the family is the first line of counseling, and it is in a safe, caring environment.

Sharing Leisure Time and Conversation

The wails and moans among parent educators, teachers, and others who work closely with children and their families often center on the decrease and perhaps extinction of quality leisure time in the family. In our zeal to provide material proof of our love for our family, we have relinquished the gift of shared time, conversation, and unstructured activities.

Television has been villianized for the erosion of family time together. However, we turned it on and left it to take our places with our children. We made it the pacifier and the babysitter. It is sobering to remember that an infant does not learn how to talk by watching television and videos. Language is taught in face-to-face interactions between a child and others. Turn the television off except for specified times that have been established with the child.

As the child grows, watch the shows with him from time to time to check out their content. The real problem with television viewing, of course, is there is no interaction, no conversation, no exchange of ideas, and no transference of family history, pride and values.

Shared leisure time is often unplanned and spontaneous activities such as a game of checkers, a search for four-leaf clovers or a walk around the block. It is in those settings that children and adults relax and talk to each other. Conversation may not happen every time, but we simply need to provide opportunities for meaningful interactions as often as possible.

Shared leisure time is often unplanned and spontaneous activities such as a game of checkers, a search for four-leaf clovers or a walk around the block.

Get up on a Saturday morning and say to an individual child, "This morning we're going to do anything you want to do that does not cost any money." Letting the child choose the activity with the understanding that it must be free sets parameters but allows room for individual preferences. Next Saturday another child gets the opportunity. Each child needs time alone with a parent to receive full attention without having to posture for a sibling. The morning activity doesn't really matter because the goal is to be together. The activity could be tossing a ball, sampling the perfume atomizers at the department store, looking at all the mitts at the mall, or just looking for tadpoles. The focus is on the relationship, not on buying one more "thing."

The amount of time is not really significant if it is truly shared. If a child has ten to fifteen minutes per day of uninterrupted time that is comfortable and treasured by both, then the relationship grows. That is why a family vacation does not compensate for a year where there has been no shared time. Letting a relationship languish for fifty-one weeks and expecting a week of vacation to reestablish the closeness is not realistic. Too much happens in the life of a child in one day, much less a week. Nevertheless, we look for a quick fix, carving out a week or so to rebuild family lines of communication. Instead, we usually return home tired, irritable, in debt and with all our clothes dirty. Spurts of time throughout the week are much more helpful, keeping us involved in the day-to-day lives of our children.

Research shows that most of what we say to children is instructions: sit down, stand up, go outside, come inside, do your homework, eat your dinner, take a bath, pick up your clothes, wash your hands, turn the TV off, answer the telephone, get off the telephone, be quiet, turn down the stereo, come here, give me a hug, brush your teeth. The list goes on and on in a given day. This is not conversation.

With children we often go into our drill sergeant, lecturer, or judge mode, giving out advice, directions, and wisdom with little feedback or response. As a matter of fact, we think that if we talk long and hard enough, the child will finally say, "Thank you, Mother, for sharing your wisdom. I fully understand what to do, thanks to you." That's just not going to happen in most situations.

One afternoon as I was cooking dinner, my son came in the kitchen and nonchalantly said, "I think they should legalize marijuana." I went off like a rocket, expounding without taking a breath, "We can't legalize marijuana. It's a gateway drug. It gets you into the drug culture. Next you'll be snoring cocaine, shooting up heroin, or sniffing glue. Marijuana saps your ambition, makes you lazy, and lowers your sperm count." Finally after thirty minutes I ran down like a clock. I expected him to say, "Now I understand. Thank you so much for imparting your wisdom." How ridiculous. I should have just said. "Why?" He really just wanted a conversation, to share something from a class at school or have an interchange of ideas. As a result I will never really know what he thought at that time.

Finding time to have a conversation with a child is something parents don't do particularly well. Conversation is an interchange of ideas, feelings and information. When we have conversations with our friends, we demonstrate respect and attention. As we watch adults converse, they look at each other, and they look interested.

There is a sense of equity in the relationship. A parent comes home tired from work and starts supper—a child wants to talk. At bedtime when the parent is looking forward to finally getting a chance to sit down—a child wants to talk. We are frequently not at our best at listening and talking at those times. However, if the parent can hold things together for five minutes, listen attentively, and respond with interest and caring on his/her face, the child learns important lessons about his place and value in the home and about his right to share his thoughts and feelings.

A need also exists for the parent to share with the child. This includes appropriately sharing disappointments of the day at work, frustrations, and feelings. This involves conversation, not venting or yelling. This models the behavior the parent wants in the child, giving the parent an opportunity to actually give names to feelings, and promote empathy in the child. There is nothing wrong with asking an older child, "What would you have done in my situation?" The child needs to understand that he does not have to find a solution (just as a parent needs to listen without feeling he must solve every problem for the child), but that his input is being invited and valued.

The conversations that are truly significant often have sentences that begin with "How", "Do you think...?", "Talk to me about....", "I'm interested in what you....", "I want to share this with you...." They encourage an interchange of feelings and ideas that is accepting, open and nonjudgmental. During this type of conversation, a parent gets to know the child. The child's activities, interests and dreams all come into the discussion. The parent gets an idea of what is really going on in the child's life, who he thinks is cool, what he thinks is fun, his perspective on life and his own values. The parent also has an opportunity to share similar thoughts.

During these shared moments, parents have a chance to catch a thought or concern from a child that is critical, but could be easily lost in the frenzy of taking care of a family's needs. These minutes allow us to know our child better than anyone else does, and we can answer personal questions such as, "What is my child most afraid of? What embarrasses my child the most? How does my child think that other people see him? Who outside the family has influenced my child the most? Does my child feel that he/she is too large or too small for his/her age? What accomplishment is my child most proud of? What would my child change about our family?" Questions like these that allow us to understand our children are answered in conversation, and conversation occurs only with shared time.

A Sense of Humor

Humor is like a salve for a rash or oil for an engine. It helps to make life bearable. The irritants, the bumps and the aches are smoothed out with a bit of humor. Healthy families have a sense of humor about themselves and life in general. Humor is *not* about ridicule, sarcasm, laughing at others, making "fun" or jest at another's expense.

> Humor involves an ability to laugh at ourselves and to see the general silliness of life.

Humor involves an ability to laugh at ourselves and to see the general silliness of life. It is critical to our ability to relax and be resilient because many times a sense of humor is our only way to cope. It eases tension and provides a medium of communication when relationships occasionally turn tense and uncomfortable. It also provides a basis for a common history for our lives. When adult children get together, someone says, "Remember that time...," and a funny story of growing up follows. It is intimate and warm to share little inside jokes and past experiences.

None of this happens, however, if we as adults do not let ourselves go and laugh at ourselves. It is a wonderfully freeing for a child to hear a parent tell a story about being horribly embarrassed or doing something silly and laughing about it. This in turn gives children permission to laugh at themselves and us, sharing fallibilities and idiosyncrasies. There is a quality of intimacy about shared humor. Children love "being in on things." Laughter in a family lasts long after children have grown up and gone. It helps to create a family fabric or history that is built on something positive and fun.

In an emotionally healthy family, everyone has warts and admits it. Perhaps there is a comparison of warts, which allows a unique bond to be shared. Laughter and shared humorous experiences go a long way in building a history for the family. These moments of shared humor weave a pleasant fabric of memories and fun that families treasure. There is nothing like trying to get in the wrong car in the shopping center while a teenage daughter sits two cars over and laughs. It's when that teenage girl comes home her senior year with her hair totally shaved off on one side with the other side long and says, "Mom, how do you like it?" It's when the playschool teacher desperately calls in the spring to inform you that your four-year-old son has kissed every girl in the class and has started around again. Each of these situations begins to build a story—a story that will later be shared starting with the phrase "Remember that time...."

A Feeling of Family

When families lived on farms, worked together, spent most of their time together and truly depended on each other, there was a bond that was critical to survival. Out of this interdependence came a sense of "family" or unity that manifested itself in pride and a feeling of being unique. In addition, most families brought customs, traditions, and special characteristics to the United States from their native countries. As our society has changed from agrarian to industrialized, with most people living in urban areas, dependence on family has greatly diminished. In our efforts to blend in and look like everyone else, distinguishing customs have been dropped. Families have lost much of their special personality and flavor.

As a result of mobility, changes in economic pursuits, divorce, and other sociological changes, children often do not have access to extended family on a regular basis. Not only has this taken a parent's backup caretaker away, it has diminished the ability of a family to pass on traditions, family lore, and customs. That makes the job of the parent to preserve this history even more challenging.

For example, there is something very satisfying when a child is able to say, "In our family we celebrate the holidays by..." to find a sense of being special. We have come to love genealogy and information about our family histories. Perhaps our days of trying to achieve the ultimate alchemy of the melting pot are over, and each of us can return to a pride in our individual family. Even families with problems and deficiencies can isolate strengths of the past to build upon.

...children need a feeling of being part of a distinct family unit that has special characteristics.

With this in mind, children need a feeling of being part of a distinct family unit that has special characteristics. If a family doesn't have special traditions, they can begin now to build these touchstones for their children. At a conference several years ago a woman asked in a question/answer session, "How can we build a sense of family when my siblings all live in different parts of the country?" I suggested that she sit down and write out a story she remembered from her childhood. The story did not have to be dramatic or even uplifting. Mail this story to a sibling, ask him or her to read it, and add a personal story or recollection and mail it to the next family member. It would not take long to build an anthology that the entire family could appreciate.

• • • • • •

All of these characteristics help to provide an environment where empathy is modeled, encouraged and valued. The family must be a safe place where a child can grow and develop in all aspects of his life and later establish a home where the same elements that promote a healthy family environment will exist.

As professionals, our inability to have time to examine, assess, and evaluate disciplinary methods in a total family context limits or even negates our ability to see long range effects or outcomes for the child.

Chapter Four

Discipline and Emotionally Healthy Children

Much of the discussion of the treatment of children revolves around the subject of discipline. Parents see discipline or child management as one of their primary, if not the most important, roles. When asked, parents will say that they are supposed to make their children "mind." Society expects parents to control their children in order to train them to be law-abiding citizens. This is an understood obligation for parents. When they do not follow through on this responsibility, people will comment on their failure to do so.

Words and phrases related to the act of discipline abound in our vocabulary, both now and in the past. Examples are: behind the woodshed, take a lickin', bend over and grab your ankles, larropin, paddling, caning, time out, spank, whop, tan, teach a lesson, tan your britches, rap your knuckles, wash your mouth out with soap, dose of castor oil, nose in a ring, stand in the corner, goofy chair, dunce hat, restriction, grounding, consequences, and a multitude of others.

The concept of appropriate discipline is based on history, cultural norms, family customs, and social mores. There is no formal list of the types of discipline with which society appears to be comfortable and will allow. However, methods of discipline that we consider child abuse or neglect are not approved by society. We set out in statute and CPS policy guidelines what a parent cannot do, but we do not provide positive guidelines for parents to follow. Until some parents are told that their methods of discipline cross a line, there is a great deal of room for misunderstanding, poor judgment, and repetition of inappropriate parenting behaviors.

As professionals, our inability to have time to examine, assess, and evaluate disciplinary methods in a total family context limits or even negates our ability to see long range effects or outcomes for the child. For example, an adult behavior taken as a one-time or isolated act could appear to be insignificant. Placed, however, within a consistent pattern of discipline and exacerbated by a lack of empathy, the same behavior could be devastating to the child.

In research focused on determining risk for child abuse, Paula Rosenstein found empathy to be the critical factor in assessment. (Rosenstein, 1995) In families where there was a high level of empathy between the caretaker and the child, there was virtually no abuse. In this study group, the ability to feel what the child felt became a governor on behavior. When a parent can feel the child's pain, it hurts the parent too much to abuse the child. Where stress has been historically regarded as the primary co-existent factor in abuse, Rosenstein's research identified the lack of parental empathy as the primary co-existent factor. She measured stress in the parents of the study group and, despite the presence of extreme stress, empathetic parents still did not abuse their children.

Dr. James Garbarino, presently professor of human development at Cornell University, suggests that society gives parents five ways to discipline their children. The methods are fear, guilt, invasion or intrusion, indulgence, and force. We can call it child management, setting limits, making them "mind" or whatever we wish. It works out much the same in the end. With all five methods parents are trying to change or limit behaviors. Each category is altered in impact according to such factors as age, personality of the child, past history of the parent-child relationship, context of the disciplinary action, frequency, and treatment of other children in the family.

There is a broad range of actions, from mild to extreme that may occur in each disciplinary method. Paula Rosenstein's research helps us understand that, while all may be used as an appropriate tool, they also can become a weapon according to intent or severity. In the hands of a non-empathetic parent or caretaker, any technique can become abusive and lead not to discipline, but to maltreatment. Empathy is the ingredient that soothes and sustains the relationship in the face of ignorance, economic pressures, stress, and basic errors in judgment or understanding. It gives a parent the motivation to learn a better way. It means that the intent of the parent was to discipline and not simply to cause hurt.

Without the presence of empathy, the relationship between child and caregiver easily moves to one where abuse under the guise of discipline thrives.

Without the presence of empathy, the relationship between child and caregiver easily moves to one where abuse under the guise of discipline thrives. In the hands of a non-empathetic parent or caretaker, any technique can become abusive. As we examine Dr. Garbarino's identified methods of discipline, we must reflect on the possible family context within which they can occur. The methods allow for a broad range of parenting behaviors, from those that are pragmatic and useful to those that are severely damaging.

Fear

Parents use fear or "scare" their children into acting in a manner they desire. On one end of the continuum, this may be a statement such as, "Don't cross the street or you may get run over." Obviously, this is seen by most people as a healthy fear that should be instilled in children since it is true, and a child's failure to listen has the potential for serious consequences. Another example of using fear that falls in this category is, "Don't be drinking after other people. You could get strep or flu." That is a statement of fact that is designed to prevent a known danger.

Taken to an extreme in the other direction, however, this method becomes an intervention that can paralyze a child, hinder appropriate development, and foster unhealthy feelings about the world—statements such as, "If you don't agree with me or back me up, you will not be a part of this family." Another statement of fear is, "Act right or your daddy will never come back." Or it may be a statement such as, "Don't argue with me, or when you get home today, I'll be gone forever."

These last statements use fear to an extreme that is harmful and cruel, using security and acceptance as a lever with a child who may already be vulnerable. Regardless, this use of fear generally goes unchecked in situations such as this, and it results in no negative response from the community. When others witness it, there may be a disapproving glance or frown, but basically nothing happens to deter this behavior. After all, nothing "really happened," and most people do not interfere with the rights of the parent. The parent is left, unchecked, to threaten, scare, and sometimes terrorize the child for his own purposes.

Guilt

This means of changing or controlling behavior in children is as old as time. Using the strength and importance of the relationship, i.e. *love*, the parent attempts to make the child "feel bad" for doing certain things. On some level this method says to a child, "If you love me or care about me, you will not do this," or "You will do this if you love me." This strategy also seeks to evoke a feeling in the child of remorse or responsibility. Words like "wrong" or "bad" may appear in these conversations, and the parent is likely to refer to moral or family standards.

At one end of the possible continuum of behaviors, there are some actions where guilt will most likely have little long-term negative effect. For example, telling a teenager, "Don't go out and act crazy. You represent our family and any one of us can make us all look bad." That's basically the truth for many situations, and it reminds the child that he or she is part of a group whose members' behavior reflects on the entire group. Guilt is the lever, but most people would agree that it is not a club. Another example, "Don't say those things. It hurts me." Guilt is once again used, but it also is a means of sharing feelings and developing empathy. Each of these is grounded in reality and reminds the child of his or her relationship to others.

> Guilt at the negative extreme of the continuum takes the form of manipulation and unhealthy use of love and affection.

Guilt at the negative extreme of the continuum takes the form of manipulation and unhealthy use of love and affection. It is used to satisfy the needs or desires of the parent rather than the best interests of the child. Statements such as, "If you love me, you won't visit your father," or "It's your fault that I'm sick," or "Don't get married and leave me. I can't make it without you." The list goes on and on where guilt is used as a weapon to control and manipulate a child. Using the strength and importance of the relationship, the parent threatens and postures to get an advantage. If the motivations of the parent are selfish or hurtful, this use of guilt becomes a weapon and is detrimental to the child's best interest.

If the effort is to control with no concern for the child's mental health, the use of guilt carries heavy baggage that, for many children, accumulates over time. The child ends up taking undeserved responsibility for the happiness or unhappiness of others.

Many adults appear to feel that they have been victimized by guilt, almost as if it is a part of life. There are many jokes about the guilt-inflicting mother, some harmless and others very hurtful. Placing this disciplinary strategy within the total context of the family allows us to see the difference between the somewhat common feelings of guilt that are humorous and inconsequential and the guilt that destroys a person's ability to move forward.

Invasion or Intrusion

This approach may be the most common and overused method because it is a means over control or intervention. Certainly we expect parents to intervene and exert control over young children since intervention is necessary for the child's safety and welfare. The young child has no sense of danger or of personal needs such as appropriate clothing and food. In the first two years of the child's life especially, the parent thinks for the child and acts accordingly.

However, even a six-month old child can choose among several toys, or show a preference for a particular fruit. As these individual tastes and feelings emerge, most parents wish to encourage the beginning of a child's autonomy. Parents start to allow children to choose clothing from a group of appropriate possibilities and decide between positive activities. As the years pass in a child's life, he develops his personal tastes and opinions. Thoughtful parents allow the child to have more independence, particularly on decisions that do not involve safety or overall welfare. The goal is that by the time a child is ready to leave home for work or college, he or she is able to think and make good decisions that will bring positive outcomes. The old phrase, "letting go of the apron strings," reflects an understanding of a child's need to move toward adulthood as the parents reduce their control over his life.

Appropriate intervention becomes intrusion when the process of control continues past the time when it is developmentally appropriate...

Appropriate intervention becomes intrusion when the process of control continues past the time when it is developmentally appropriate, resulting in a squelching of the child's personality and interfering with his move toward autonomy and independence. The parent may continue to control every part of the child's life, including his friends, activities, thoughts, and opinions, making all decisions and overriding the child's feelings. The parent may intrude into the child's life to the extent that a child has no ability to make decisions.

Realizing that children make better decisions when they have preparation and practice, Parents and Children Together (PACT) in

Decatur, Alabama, developed a mini-course for fifth graders on decision-making skills. The course included a discussion of the process of evaluating the situation, identifying possible alternatives and determining the consequences of each alternative. This process of thought and caution was placed in the curriculum to give children some necessary skills they need to deal with drugs or sexual pressures. However, one parent objected to the discussion of problem solving and decision-making and took her child from the class. Her justification was that, "I will tell my child exactly what to do, and she (the child) will have no need to make a decision." Of course, a thoughtful parent who understands the child's journey toward maturity realizes that life-changing decisions are not made when the parent is present. Nevertheless, this parent wanted to hold onto control even though it flies in the face of healthy emotional development.

When invasion is used to an extreme as a child management intervention, it becomes a type of mind control...

When invasion is used to an extreme as a child management intervention, it becomes a type of mind control where the parent is determined to make all decisions involving the child and controls the child's interactions with the world. This child leaves home at eighteen with absolutely no experience in looking at possibilities, evaluating consequences and making decisions. This intervention, coupled often with fear, is extremely harmful to a healthy process of learning and development for a child. It definitely interferes with elements of emotional intelligence such as confidence and curiosity.

The first eighteen years of a person's life should be a journey of growth where a parent thoughtfully expands the opportunities for a child to develop autonomy in a safe and caring environment. It starts in infancy where a child is unable to make decisions except when to eat or sleep and hopefully will end with maturity and self-sufficiency and an ability to make appropriate choices. The parent's ability to encourage independence in small increments, based on the child's abilities, is actually an exercise in discipline for both the parent and the child.

Indulgence

This child management technique has been the product, for the most part, of a more advantaged society. We have more material benefits, namely available money to spend, and these material possibilities are translated into "perks" parents offer to children in return for desired outcomes or behaviors. In other words, parents often "buy" the child with money, activities, trips, clothes, cars, or other luxury items.

Indulgence as a parenting tool may have also been a product of overzealousness or misuse of the behavior modification principles of the '60's. Many parents have taken the ideas of that model, adapted them, perhaps adulterated them, and ended up with a loose, bartering system in the family where the child must be paid for behaviors that should merely be expected from an emotionally healthy, caring person. Everything has a price tag, and the parent must pay.

Other appropriate uses of indulgence may be similar to adults' bonus system at work where extra, unrequired effort is rewarded.

No one can take real issue with a mild use of indulgence. There is nothing wrong with using M&M's® to reinforce the use of the commode by a two-year-old child saying, "Make bubbles and Mommy will give you an M&M®." Other appropriate uses of indulgence may be similar to adults' bonus system at work where extra, unrequired effort is rewarded. A child may contract with the parent to clean the gutters or paint the house instead of employing an outsider. Basing a weekly allowance on a series of chores or responsibilities is technically using indulgence since payment of an allowance is not required; however, this practice can teach many valuable principles regarding the value of work, especially if the money is not paid when chores are half done or the child must be nagged or chronically reminded.

Extreme indulgence, such as paying for good conduct grades, buying expensive cars to gain the affection of a child, or trying to control a child's personal behavior with credit cards, excessive allowances or clothes occurs for any of several reasons. The parent may be a person who "came up hard" and wants his child to have "everything he didn't." In some situations the parent wants desperately to be the child's friend or buddy, and buying is one way to gain approval from the child. By going down this road, the parent abdicates his primary roles as parent, guide, and supervisor, but justifies his conduct by feeling that he is making the child "happy." On the other hand, some parents are just too lazy to go to all the thought, effort, and work it takes to plan positive disciplinary strategies, place them in motion, monitor them carefully and follow up appropriately and as promised. Regardless of which reason is the impetus behind the use of indulgence as discipline, it is most assuredly facilitated by the availability of excess money or credit that earlier generations did not have.

No other means of discipline has evoked more discussion and regulation than the use of force.

When the child grows bigger and is not easily controlled by force, guilt, or fear, the parent sees indulgence as perhaps the last line of defense against a total lack of control. The indulging parent uses family resources to avoid holding the line and saying "no" when faced with a strong-willed adolescent.

Force

No other means of discipline has evoked more discussion and regulation than the use of force. It is seen by many to be synonymous with discipline. The other four types are merely seen as parental behaviors or techniques.

Given that a child is physically smaller than the parent, and the feeling that the will and/or wisdom of the parent should prevail, physical force has historically been the primary way parents control children. It requires little thought or explanation, and it represents the method most parents experienced themselves as children, making the action feel familiar and proven.

Force is immediate, active and has been historically institutionalized and approved. As a rule, it allows the parent to feel as if he or she has done something tangible to correct the behavior. A statement has been made to the child and any other person who witnesses it, and the parent can feel that parental responsibility has been met.

The term "child abuse" came into our lexicon to define the inappropriate use of force, yet few agree on exactly what that term really means.

Over the last forty years the use of physical force has been examined, argued about, and the subject of many state laws. The term "child abuse" came into our lexicon to define the inappropriate use of force, yet few agree on exactly what that term really means. Definitions are subjective at best, and appear to change depending on the legal or political environment. From a legal perspective, most state statutes use terms such as "imminent danger" or "life-threatening danger" as the standard for outside intervention. Every other use of force, which generally is unaddressed by outside authority, may fall along a continuum from what some refer to as "normal spanking" to "poor parenting techniques" involving frequent and harsh physical punishment. Some parents even believe it is impossible to be a good parent if physical punishment is not used, citing, "Spare the rod and spoil the child." The use of force for child management, although not accepted by some, continues to be a common intervention allowed in all states.

The use of institutionalized corporal punishment in school, residential care facilities, and other child caring institutions, is prohibited in over one-half of the states and many other local school districts, indicating the concern lawmakers and policy makers have had for the use of force by non-related persons. State-licensed foster parents are generally prohibited from using corporal punishment on the foster children in their care. This is certainly ironic, given the fact that generally when a child is returned to what has been determined as abusive parents, the parents may use corporal punishment.

Despite these major changes, there are still those who lobby for the return of corporal punishment to schools. There have been situations where supposedly enlightened parents attempt to coerce schools to reinstate paddling despite the fact that it has been banned for decades. There is a real anomaly between a school's attempts to put an end to violent behavior and fighting among its students by using the discipline of spanking and force. What does a student do with the message, "I can't hit someone, but you can hit me?"

What does a student do with the message, "I can't hit someone, but you can hit me?"

The opinions of some parents about the use of force or corporal punishment have changed over the last twenty years as parents have examined their parenting practices, sought effective and appropriate alternatives, and learned more about child development. The American Academy of Pediatrics has taken a position against the use of corporal punishment by parents. In addition, our general attitudes about physical force or violence have changed. Where fighting among adults in the street, workplace, or other public areas was once accepted, it is now generally disapproved. Oddly enough, most of the violence we see today occurs in the home, either between spouses, boyfriend and girlfriend, or administered upon children as punishment. Otherwise, we have pronounced violence as unacceptable.

Force or corporal punishment for some parents simply means taking a two year old child's hands when she touches a crystal vase and lightly slapping them while saying, "No!" That, along with a swat or two on the buttocks when the child tries to cross the street or pull the dog's tail, may be the only time a parent uses force. In cases such as these, the parent is using force to either get the attention of the child and/or as a means to alter behavior until the child is more able to respond to reason. Causing pain does not appear to be part of the equation.

The use of force has broad, far-reaching manifestations, all of which are generally allowed by our society at this time. Whippings with belts, paddles, and switches are common and unregulated unless the outcome is "injury" such as marks or bruises. Corporal punishment is seen by some as a parental right or choice, even if parents spank every night to make children go to bed, or administer "licks" for everything. Force as an intervention varies among families like no other means of discipline. Some parents see no problem with slapping the face, pinching, shaking, using duct tape, washing mouths out with soap, administering multiple "licks" based on the offense, or placing a child in the isolation of a closet.

Corporal punishment is seen by some as a parental right or choice, even if parents spank every night to make children go to bed, or administer "licks" for everything.

All of these uses of force, although not viewed by many as "good parenting," constitute what some parents see as their parental rights, even duty. Again, the spanking administered by an empathetic parent who says, "This hurts me more than it hurts you," will normally not become punishment that damages the emotional development of a child. Force used by a nonempathetic parent will always have the potential to cross the line into abuse.

• • • • • •

The Concept of Positive Discipline

Discipline in the form of punishment is generally regulated by what a parent *should not* or *cannot* do. Society does not normally set boundaries establishing what a parent *should* do. However, the parent who is empathetic will benefit from a discussion of positive, practical strategies for discipline. Positive discipline is teaching. It is a process that requires the attention and time of the parent and encourages the development of empathy in the child. The negative behavior must be explained, probably many times, with emphasis on the effect it had on others. We must explain why it is unacceptable in terms the child understands. We must point out the feelings of others as a result of the behavior. Our goal is to bring the child to a point of understanding his or her behavior as it relates to others. Only then should negative consequences be applied. We want the child to be able to step up, acknowledge the infraction and try to improve. Otherwise, punishment cannot only be useless in changing behavior; it can promote bitterness, anger, and "acting out" behaviors.

When discipline is seen as a teaching process, there will be a natural move away from the use of physical or corporal punishment.

When discipline is seen as a teaching process, there will be a natural move away from the use of physical or corporal punishment. Spanking is a quick fix for most parents. It is a reaction to our own anger and our need to take action. If we can adopt a teaching approach to discipline, taking time to work through each step, then other alternatives become logical.

A two-year-old reaches for a glass candle holder on the coffee table. His mother says, "Sanders, no!" He looks at her and continues to touch the candlestick. Again she says, "No, Sanders. That belongs to Buddie, and you might break it!" He starts to pick it up. This time, his mother walks over to him, gets down on his level, looks at him directly in his eyes and says, "Do you want to go to your room?" The look on his face reflects his thoughts as he considers this. He says, "No," and moves away. Of course, his "room" is not even in that house, but he knew exactly what the potential punishment meant based on his experiences of the past. His reaction reflected the learning or discipline that had occurred before.

The following list of suggestions about the process of positive discipline is certainly not exhaustive. It does, however, reflect a healthy approach to discipline that will promote the development of Goleman's elements of emotional intelligence. The goal is to foster empathy within the context of discipline.

The Process of Positive Discipline

1. Set no more rules than necessary. Obviously, the number is greater for very small children, but will decrease with age as the child learns to limit his or her own behavior.
2. Discuss rules in advance with input by the entire family as appropriate. The rules may be placed on the refrigerator to emphasize the importance of the agreement. The American colonists rebelled against England for many reasons. One was their anger over *ex post facto* laws—new laws enforced on individuals who had broken the law before it was even enacted. We need to know in advance what is expected of us.

Ask all family members to give their opinions as to the consequence for breaking the rule.

3. Explain the need for the rule.
4. Ask all family members to give their opinions as to the consequence for breaking the rule. When the consequence is decided, add that to the document.

5. Apply the rules as consistently and fairly as possible. Our fatigue, distractions or emotional state should not get in the way of fairness.
6. Don't wait for the rule to be broken to have discussions. When the rule is followed or obeyed, acknowledge this and praise the child for compliance.
7. Control your anger when the child breaks the rule.
8. Try to understand the child's feelings and position, even if they are not appropriate.
9. Set routines for meals, bedtimes, chores, and homework. This establishes a rhythm or pattern that makes life more predictable for children.
10. Model self-control for children. Allow them to see you are concerned, upset, or frustrated, but that you act appropriately even in those situations.
11. Apologize if you lash out.
12. Tell your child, "I love you," every day.

All of these steps in the process of positive discipline help to promote the elements of emotional health and respect the true meaning of discipline, which is "to train" or "to teach." No one will dispute that it takes more time and effort to apply positive discipline. It is not a quick fix or an impulsive response. The desirable results, self-control and empathy, will not occur overnight. However, if parents begin to work with their child ages birth to five, they are likely to have a good result.

No one will dispute that it takes more time and effort to apply positive discipline.

Children who have not been able to develop healthy attachments with their caregivers, and whose early emotional experiences have not laid the necessary groundwork for healthy emotional development, may have a limited capacity for empathy.

Chapter Five

An Overview of Emotional Maltreatment

Classifying Harm and an Empathetic Deficit

The difference between coarse and refined abuse
is the difference between being bruised by
a club and wounded by a poisonous arrow.
—Samuel Johnson

Having established a framework for understanding what is needed for emotional health, it is time to look at the other side of the coin. For our purposes, the antithesis of emotional health will be called emotional maltreatment, or what Samuel Johnson calls the "poisonous arrow." The primary function of parents is to provide a setting where the child can grow, thrive, and reach adulthood ready to become a positive, contributing member of society. Those parental behaviors that prevent appropriate emotional development and health will be categorized as abuse or neglect.

Taking into consideration the diversity of families, we must be willing to pick up this sensitive subject and examine it with the welfare of children in mind.

Perhaps we can begin by examining the personal emotional scars that we have carried from childhood, the ones we remember with pain. They will be easy to find. Ask the question why the incident caused such hurt. Think about how we felt when it happened and how we responded. This self-examination will hopefully get us back into thinking and feeling like a child, remembering the child we were and the children we know now. This will create a common understanding and allow us to proceed with a dialogue.

Let's acknowledge that all of us have been victims of some degree of emotional maltreatment, and all of us who have cared for children have emotionally maltreated them in some way, either inadvertently or through inaction. In interactions with children, adults seldom really stop to analyze and reflect on the impact of words, attitudes, and actions that do not constitute physical abuse or sexual contact. In other words, we comfort ourselves that since we did not hit, slap, or molest, anything else is all right, or at least adequate. It is very uncomfortable for us to examine the emotional context of adult-child interaction, for we know we would have to change many of our behaviors.

...a lack of empathy on the part of the caretaker is the most significant common denominator in all forms of child abuse.

As we have seen, a lack of empathy on the part of the caretaker is the most significant common denominator in all forms of child abuse. Emotional maltreatment shares that characteristic with both physical and sexual abuse. It is this lack of empathy that puts the child at risk. Therefore, the presence of empathy in the family, beginning with the parents or caretakers, not only becomes the fabric of nurturance; it also becomes the deterrent to child abuse. As early experts such as Anna Freud and Erik Erikson pointed out, children need more than just food, clothing and shelter to successfully achieve the developmental stages necessary for normal adulthood. They require an environment that provides empathy and emotional nurturance. Children are born with a capacity for empathy, but unless it is nurtured, it will not develop. Empathy does not just happen in a vacuum. Empathy grows where empathy has been demonstrated to a child and encouraged by his caregivers.

Emotionally abusive and neglectful behaviors reflect an absence of empathy, the ability of the parent to feel the pain of the child. Daniel Stern, a psychiatrist at Cornell University, refers to an emotional relationship between parent and child called *attunement*. Dr. Stern defined this occurrence as intimate moments between parent and child where repeated exchanges become the most basic lessons of emotional life. He believes that of all such moments, the most critical are those that let the child know that his/her emotions are met with empathy, accepted and reciprocated in a process. This is the process of attunement. (Stern, 1987) The foundation for attunement, the interchange of empathy, is not made in these emotionally abusive relationships.

"Prolonged absence of attunement between parent and child takes a tremendous emotional toll on the child. When a parent consistently fails to show any empathy with a particular range of emotion in the child—joys, tears, needing to cuddle—the child begins to avoid expressing, and perhaps even feeling those same emotions." (Goleman, 1995) Without feeling these emotions, the grounding of empathy in the child, this child does not have the tools to interact with others in an empathetic manner.

Children who are raised without empathy shown to them and encouraged in them have the potential for causing great destruction.

Children who are raised without empathy shown to them and encouraged in them have the potential for causing great destruction. The following statement is made in *Raising Cain*. "Every troubled boy has a different story, but their stories share a disturbing theme of emotional ignorance and isolation." (Kindlon &Thompson, 1999) The authors have effectively connected the absence of an emotionally healthy environment for boys with outcomes that are aggressive and harmful to themselves and others.

"Children who have not been able to develop healthy attachments with their caregivers, and whose early emotional experiences have not laid the necessary groundwork for healthy emotional development, may have a limited capacity for empathy. The ability to feel remorse and empathy are built on experience. In the extreme, if a child feels no emotional attachment to any human being, he can not be expected to feel remorse for hurting or even killing someone." Perry offers the example of a 15-year-old who felt no remorse for having committed murder. The boy had been neglected and humiliated by his primary caretakers as a child. "He is literally emotionally retarded. The part of his brain that would have allowed him to feel connected to other human beings—empathy—simply did not develop.'" (U.S. Department of Health and Human Services, 2001)

A 1998 *USA Today* headline reads: "Lack of empathy seen as key to spotting troubled youths." Reporter Kathy S. Peterson writes of four young men between the ages of eleven and sixteen who went onto their school campuses and killed one or more of their classmates. The journalist uses such terms as "no pity", "cannot feel", "don't have sympathy", "no remorse", and "isolated" to describe these youth. She quotes Dr. Lawrence Stone, a San Antonio, Texas child psychiatrist, as saying that children who have never developed empathy "cannot feel that another is a real person as they are. When they hurt someone, they just don't register it is wrong."

The boys discussed in this article killed twelve people and injured many others. They were going to school regularly, functioning to some degree in society, yet each was a time bomb or satchel charge waiting to explode. When and why these satchel charges had been planted is unclear. It is obvious, nevertheless, that an empathetic deficit is part of the harm incurred by a child who has been emotionally abused or neglected.

They were going to school regularly, functioning to some degree in society, yet each was a time bomb or satchel charge waiting to explode.

In these graphic examples, it is obvious how emotional maltreatment has harmed the children and the people around them. However, how do we define and categorize the injury and harm experienced by a child who has been emotionally maltreated but has not, as yet, committed a heinous crime? Do we merely wait for the explosion in the child's behavior before we attend to the problem? Do we have a standard for determining harm that places a community at risk?

...how do we define and categorize the injury and harm experienced by a child who has been emotionally maltreated but has not, as yet, committed a heinous crime?

Accepted practice involving child abuse and neglect has historically focused on the measurement of injury caused by the abuse. The legal system is accustomed to looking at damage or harm as a means of determining what relief to prescribe. Evidence of physical abuse is typically a matter of counting and verifying marks or physical injuries. Sexual abuse is primarily determined by experts who can confirm the sexual contact did occur. Although sexual abuse should include any type of behavior where an adult receives sexual gratification from a child even if there is no physical touching, the easiest cases to bring into court are those which, again, involve evidence of some physical signs of contact such as genital tearing, the presence of semen, or sexually transmitted diseases.

Thus we have our dilemma with emotional abuse which, by definition, does not cause visible, physical scars. In the investigation, treatment and disposition of cases involving emotional abuse and neglect, we have not yet established recognized criteria or standards for determining either the immediate harm or the long-term damage to the child as a result of the abusive behaviors. This failure to address the subject of emotional maltreatment, set case standards, and seek relief for the child who is being harmed has resulted in a situation where the subject is commonly ignored. We have not known what to do; therefore, we have done practically nothing.

The logical place to start is to suggest a definition of "harm" or "injury." As we will discuss in another chapter, states variously define emotional injury. However, the best statutory definition is one that defines "emotional" or "mental" injury as damage or risk of damage to the psychological capacity or stability of a child that substantially impairs or threatens to impair the child's ability to function within a normal range of performance. (See Chapter Six.) This definition provides a starting place for this discussion of harm.

Good practice and basic knowledge of child development tell us that children who experience the types of abuse that we will discuss in the following chapters will incur damage. This definition of emotional damage turns the spotlight firmly on a child, focusing on how that child is performing at present and evaluating how he is most likely to function in the future. Being able to evaluate "risk" of psychological damage and "threat" to normal function allows us to go beyond immediate harm as the only measure of abuse. Concentrating just on present damage and injury cannot only be shortsighted, but dangerous over the lifetime of a child.

Being able to evaluate "risk" of psychological damage and "threat" to normal function allows us to go beyond immediate harm as the only measure of abuse.

As we begin to establish a framework within which to categorize the harm done to a child who experiences emotional maltreatment, we will first take a look at the two types of abusive behaviors directed at the child—emotional abuse and emotional neglect.

Emotional Abuse

This form of child abuse is defined here as harm committed by adults upon a child that impedes a healthy emotional development, i.e. an act or behavior of an adult toward a child or in the presence of a child that injures. The adult commits an emotionally abusive act in the same way a parent commits a physically abusive act.

In many situations where two or more adults are in the home, emotional abuse may encompass both the abusive act itself and the failure to stop the abuse. Emotional abuse can be an act of "commission" where the caretaker carries out the abusive behavior. It can also be an act of "omission" where there is a failure on the part of an adult to prevent abusive behaviors being directed at the child.

Emotional abuse can be an act of "commission" where the caretaker carries out the abusive behavior.

For example, a parent who consistently denigrates a girl by calling her "slut" and "whore" is being emotionally abusive. However, a parent is also being emotionally abusive if he/she fails to protect the child from someone who persists in saying those same things. In another example, a parent who forces a child to stay in his room and keeps him isolated from the world for an unhealthy and inappropriate period of time is being abusive. If there is another adult in the home who acquiesces and raises no objection to this punishment, that adult is being abusive because the failure to object allows the infliction of emotional harm.

Many states also include within their emotional abuse definitions situations where the caretaker creates or allows to be created a risk of emotional injury. This definition would cover a situation where a parent exposes a child to a terrifying or corrupting experience or permits another person to similarly expose the child. Normal experience tells us that taking a child on a trip at night to buy drugs creates a risk of emotional damage. Sending the child with a boyfriend on a drug-buying trip is allowing the creation of such a risk. Watching a pornographic picture with a six-year-old creates a risk of emotional harm. Not interceding when a young child watches such a film with a boyfriend or other adult is allowing the creation of the risk.

Emotional Neglect

Like neglect in general, this form of child abuse is a passive harm where the adult fails to act in an appropriate manner or else fails to provide for the child's emotional needs. It can best be understood in comparison with physical neglect, which we generally define as the failure to provide necessary food, clothing, and shelter. Medical neglect, which involves the failure to provide necessary medical care, is another form of neglect.

Emotional neglect … is the failure to provide the necessary emotional care and nurturance for a child's healthy development.

Emotional neglect, by the same token, is the failure to provide the necessary emotional care and nurturance for a child's healthy development. Although some courts consider neglect to be defined as "failing to act," we place those behaviors on the abuse side of the equation. Instead of a failure to act to prevent emotional harm, neglect is a term that references a broad range of parental failures. Abuse is frequently a matter of poor, inappropriate, or non-empathetic parenting. Neglect is more a matter of no parenting or minimal parenting.

Emotional neglect covers those parents who, frequently because of their own mental health problems or addictions, are incapable of interacting with their children in any appropriate or meaningful way. This child is not held, comforted when upset, smiled at or talked to. The parent has no realistic understanding of what to expect with regard to child development and, accordingly, does not appropriately interact to encourage the child's growth. The parent typically creates an environment that is chaotic and unpredictable and where the needs of the child are certainly not a priority.

Failure to provide for emotional needs, although a passive harm, leaves the child lacking sustenance for his emotional health, an important part of his overall health.

Given our current level of understanding regarding the impact of environment and relationships on the development of a child, it would be as heartless for us to ignore emotional needs as it would be to deny food and water. Failure to provide for emotional needs, although a passive harm, leaves the child lacking sustenance for his emotional health, an important part of his overall health. Indeed, researchers in the field of brain research express a greater concern for children who are emotionally neglected than for those who are emotionally abused.

Levels of Emotional Maltreatment

Whether a child has been emotionally damaged by abuse or neglect, we need to determine and categorize the amount of harm that has occurred. If the goal of the community is to provide services and support for children and families where children can stay in their own homes, we can define several levels of harm that will help us determine the level of outside intervention necessary to protect the child. The basic question to be answered is, "How much damage has occurred to the emotional stability of the child, and how much has the child's ability to function normally been impaired?"

The assessment process would involve interviews with the child and his parents or caretakers, interviews with the child's siblings, home visits to observe family dynamics and evaluating the child with appropriate psychological testing. Based on all of these indicators, the level of emotional harm would be classified as mild, moderate, and severe. The classification and analysis process would determine the need and level of services required.

There is no attempt here to imply that children fall into levels based on definite outcomes. Some children, of course, will be more resilient in the face of abuse by virtue of their personalities or extended support systems; however, we do not have a method of determining this. As we have discussed earlier, there appears to be such a delay in outcome that it would be impossible to completely predict any one child's level of harm from emotional abuse and neglect. Rather, the suggestion is that we begin to look, examine, and think about reasons for the behaviors we see. These behaviors do not have to be aggressive or disruptive, for the child may be quiet and withdrawn. However, when the child does not appear to be developing emotionally according to good practice standards, all professionals should begin to ask questions about the child's total environment.

Mild Emotional Maltreatment

When mild emotional maltreatment has occurred, although the child experiences emotional abuse or neglect, he or she is able to function in an adequate manner without treatment or intervention. Although most people experience some degree of emotional maltreatment, they are able to function adequately. Some children are able to adapt to mild emotional maltreatment and postpone or never manifest identifiable damage. In the first place, a child may be unusually resilient and build stronger defenses, which are appropriate to his/her long-term development and adjustment. Secondly, despite the fact that there are resulting problems from

Although most people experience some degree of emotional maltreatment, they are able to function adequately.

the emotional maltreatment, the child may internalize the damage, and postpone the destructive behaviors to a future time when he or she is faced with the stress of adolescence and adulthood.

At this level of harm, the child would remain in the home. However, the family could avail itself of community resources such as parenting seminars, parent support groups, or other education programs.

Moderate Emotional Maltreatment

A child who is the victim of moderate emotional maltreatment may call attention to himself with a variety of behaviors, attitudes, and deficiencies that adults tend to address. These may include debilitating shyness, withdrawal or compulsive behaviors. These behaviors may cause discomfort to others, be disruptive, or evoke concern and empathy from teachers or other adults. These behaviors usually trigger an investigation into the reasons for the unacceptable conduct. The child probably cannot or will not give a verbal reason on his own for the causes of his actions. He may not see the parental behavior as unusual, or with misplaced loyalty he is willing to endure anything to protect and maintain the family together. In other cases the child, especially the oldest child, in a seriously dysfunctional family learns very early in life to just "take it."

A child who is the victim of moderate emotional maltreatment may call attention to himself with a variety of behaviors, attitudes, and deficiencies that adults tend to address.

Parents may seek counseling for a child because he is an oppositional, sullen, belligerent, or "impossible to deal with." Teachers notice these children because their behaviors disrupt the learning process for themselves and others. At this point a guidance counselor may ask parental permission for a child to be evaluated for possible placement in special education. There may or may not be a referral for outside counseling. Some school systems are reluctant to make referrals since they could be financially liable for the cost of such services. At this point, it might be appropriate for a teacher to make a referral to CPS.

Because the child has been identified as not functioning at a normal performance level, outside intervention such as counseling, mental health therapy or special education is required. The child is, however, able to remain in his own home. A plan needs to be implemented and the family system monitored carefully to determine whether a more rigorous intervention is needed to protect the child from more severe emotional abuse or neglect.

Severe Emotional Maltreatment

In the case of severe emotional maltreatment, time is critical. This child who may be cowed at home can turn into the aggressor or tormentor outside the home. The object of his aggression may be animals or smaller, vulnerable children. Although it may begin with name-calling, bullying, ridicule, or put-downs, it can progress into more dangerous behaviors if left unchecked. It is important to note that merely identifying a child as having severe emotional or mental problems, without looking for the cause, does not solve the problem. In the case of emotional maltreatment, the child may be left in the very situation that is causing the problem.

The damage incurred by child abuse is generally proportionate to the closeness and importance of the relationship that the child has with the abuser.

The impact of severe emotional abuse or neglect necessitates or probably should necessitate the placement of the child in residential treatment, therapeutic foster care, or some other out-of-home care. The damage incurred by child abuse is generally proportionate to the closeness and importance of the relationship that the child has with the abuser. This is the reason that abuse within the family, where ties are close and the child is greatly emotionally invested, is the most damaging. In cases of severe maltreatment, where there may be malicious intent, total parental apathy or inadequacy and an absence of empathy, the damage can be great. This serious situation is usually accompanied by the parent's lack of cooperation or even hostility toward the CPS agency that negates their ability to effectively intervene. Because of these extreme circumstances, removal of the child from the home may be the only way to ensure his safety and provide intensive treatment for him and the family.

In these extremely serious cases, where the CPS worker does not have the presence of parental empathy on which to draw to provoke changes and change, there may be no governor on the parent's behavior, and intervention without removal can easily place the child at more serious risk.

As with physical abuse and sexual abuse, the first step in dealing with emotional maltreatment is to look truthfully at the problem, regardless of how complex or pervasive it is.

• • • • • •

As with physical abuse and sexual abuse, the first step in dealing with emotional maltreatment is to look truthfully at the problem, regardless of how complex or pervasive it is. Acknowledging its identity and understanding the seriousness of harm done to children will force us to begin the journey to resolution. As long as we ignore emotional maltreatment, we don't have to struggle with solutions. However, as we begin this journey of understanding and action, we will come to terms with the problem, determine its extent, create a plan to address it, and embark on creating community standards that will help to prevent it.

By not generally making abuse a crime pursued by law enforcement, the problem of child maltreatment was, and to a large extent remains, discounted.

CHAPTER SIX

Statutory Definitions of Emotional Maltreatment

Statutory changes to protect children from abuse and neglect occurred in the 1970's. After a full decade of discussing individual rights, both for minorities and women, our attention finally turned to children and their lack of established rights. Since children need someone else to speak for them, do not as a rule file lawsuits, vote, organize demonstrations, and negatively impact the marketplace with boycotts, it is predictable that their rights would be addressed last. Although some states had statutes regarding child abuse, there was no uniform code or approach to a problem that was seen as very limited in scope and perhaps an invasion of the home and family.

The lack of attention and concern for this problem is probably reflected in the legal approach states had used to address it. Child Welfare Bureaus were a part of the overall public welfare system that included commodities, old-age pensions, aid to the disabled and blind, and aid for families lacking parental support. The bureaus prior to the 1970's primarily handled adoptions and maintained foster care for children left orphaned or abandoned. Since the child welfare system had homes in which to place children, this became the logical system to have responsibility for child abuse. By placing primary responsibility with the welfare system, the states perhaps inadvertently identified child abuse with the most disadvantaged sector of the community. By not generally making abuse a crime pursued by law enforcement, the problem of child maltreatment was, and to a large extent remains, discounted. It has taken years and great harm to children to move the violence done to children away from one merely regarded as a "do-gooder's" issue.

However, in the mid '70's, federal requirements for state child abuse statutes were enacted that included the establishment of central registries for reporting abuse, designation of mandatory reporters, and stipulations for the inclusion of child abuse in state statute. Things began to change. State legislatures rewrote the language of their laws, and child protective service agencies revised policy and procedures to conform to federal guidelines.

Although initially most states defined their mandatory reporting laws on child abuse only in terms of physical and sexual abuse, the later enactment by the federal government of the Child Abuse Prevention and Treatment Act (CAPTA) in 1988 required each state to include a definition of "emotional harm" in its abuse and neglect reporting statutes in order to qualify for certain federal dollars. In reality, the word "emotional" slid into law without a great deal of notice or attention. Certainly the same effort to address emotional abuse, as we have done with its counterparts physical and sexual abuse, has never happened.

Since 1996, CAPTA requires states to *minimally* define child abuse and neglect to include "any recent act or failure to act of a parent or caretaker," which results in "serious physical or *emotional harm*" or "an act or failure to act which presents an imminent risk of serious harm." (42 U.S.C. § 5106 g (2)) There are several essential elements in the CAPTA "minimal" definition of emotional harm that are of critical significance as we move forward with addressing emotional maltreatment on the institutional level. These elements address abuse and neglect issues that persistently crop up involving intent, passive abuse and the concept of imminent danger. The 1996 language, intentionally or not,

[2]Until the language changed in 1996, CAPTA defined "child abuse and neglect" as "the physical or *mental injury*, sexual abuse or exploitation, negligent treatment, or maltreatment of a child by a person who is responsible for the child's welfare, under circumstances which indicate that the child's health or welfare is harmed or threatened thereby..." (Emphasis supplied)

reflects the development of new information and understanding regarding the emotional needs of children.[2]

The three elements addressed are:

- First, the CAPTA standard deals with *serious emotional harm,* whether there is *present* harm or *imminent risk* of such harm.
- Second, a caretaker's *failure* to act, not just his/her actions, can cause emotional harm.
- Third, the concern is whether the act or failure to act *results* in serious emotional harm.

Several things are significant about the new language. The focus of our interest is placed squarely on the impact and effect of abuse on the child, *not* on whether the caretaker deliberately inflicted emotional harm or whether there was an "intent" to cause the injury. In addition, not only are we not concerned with whether the parent or caretaker knew his *actions* would cause emotional harm, we will become involved when his *failure to act* causes harm. In other words, caretakers who passively allow harm to children will be held responsible in an abuse and neglect investigation. Finally, and probably most important, the focus of our concern is whether the child is suffering "serious emotional harm" or whether there is an "imminent" *risk* of such harm. The CAPTA language clarifies that, with regard to emotional maltreatment, the "imminent" standard for intervention is not focused on whether a child's life is in danger, but whether his emotional well being is in serious jeopardy.

The focus of our interest is placed squarely on the impact and effect of abuse on the child, not on whether the caretaker deliberately inflicted emotional harm....

Unfortunately, CAPTA does not require states to enact specific statutory language, and, accordingly, states vary widely in the manner in which the emotional portion of their abuse and neglect laws is defined. States variously refer to emotional harm in their abuse and neglect statutes not only by that term, but also by "mental injury," "emotional maltreatment", "psychological harm", or "emotional injury." Some limit the reference to just the phrase, while others include an expanded definition, standards for determination, and requirements for intervention. Some definitions contained in statutory language do not come close to conforming to the minimal standards set by CAPTA. In fact, there are still three states that do not include emotional abuse in their abuse and neglect reporting statutes. A review of all of these variations in statutory language follows.

Statutes Conforming to CAPTA Requirements

The best and most thorough definition of emotional harm is model language found in approximately one-third of the states. Typical of this language is the Kentucky child abuse reporting statute. The statute first identifies an abused or neglected child as one whose health and welfare is harmed or threatened when his custodian inflicts or allows to be inflicted emotional injury or creates or allows to be created a risk of emotional injury. The statutory language then defines "emotional injury" as:

> an injury to the mental or psychological capacity or emotional stability of a child as evidenced by a substantial and observable impairment in the child's ability to function within a normal range of performance and behavior with due regard to his age, development, culture, and environment as testified to by a qualified mental health professional. Ky. Rev. Stat. Ann. § 600.020(24).

The Kentucky statute contains all of the factors required by CAPTA. First, "emotional harm" is defined as a substantial impairment of a child's ability to function. Second, the responsibility of a caretaker includes a failure to act to prevent an emotional injury. Third, the focus is on the impact of the caretaker's behavior on the child, not on whether the caretaker intended to emotionally injure the child.

Kentucky does require that the emotional injury was inflicted other than by accidental means. This, however, does not mean the caretaker must have intended to damage the child. Instead, the question is whether there has been a pattern of injurious behavior by the parent or custodian. A parent will not be found to be abusive on the basis of a one-time behavior. Once an investigation determines that the behavior (whether in physical or emotional abuse cases) has occurred repetitively, it is no longer "accidental," regardless of whether the caretaker intended to cause an emotional injury.

Kentucky's statute also includes two factors frequently found in states having similar definitions of emotional or mental injury in their abuse and neglect statutes. First, states require that the culture within which the child is being raised be taken into account in determining whether the actions or inactions of the caretaker would constitute emotional abuse. Second, it is not unusual for a statute to require an evaluation and opinion by a mental health professional confirming that a substantial injury to a child's mental or psychological status has occurred. Since emotional abuse does not involve physical scars or signs, many legislators have placed within the statute a requirement of validation of the psychological damage by a professional. Some states, either through a specific statutory requirement or through policy enactments, require two professionals. Usually this involves opinions supplied by a caseworker and a psychiatrist or psychologist.

Since emotional abuse does not involve physical scars or signs, many legislators have placed within the statute a requirement of validation of the psychological damage by a professional.

The most important aspect of this language is that it leaves no doubt that the focus of the investigation and diagnosis is on the child, not on the parent. Indeed, this definition settles the issue of what will be the focus in determining whether a child has been emotionally abused or neglected. Since "injury" is defined as impairment to the child's ability to function psychologically and emotionally within a normal range, the parent's "intent" to cause harm or failure to understand the effect of his/her behaviors is not to be considered. Instead, the effect of those behaviors on the child will be the foundation for evaluation and investigation.

States that have enacted all or a part of this model language are: Alaska, Arkansas, Colorado, Florida, Hawaii, Iowa, Maine, Maryland, Montana, Nevada, South Carolina, South Dakota, Tennessee, Texas, Wisconsin and Wyoming.

Another third of the states include emotional abuse (in any of its various terms) in their abuse and neglect statutes, but provide no additional definition of the term. Missouri, for example, defines "abuse" to mean "physical injury, sexual abuse, or emotional abuse inflicted on a child other than by accidental means by those responsible for the child's care, custody, and control." (Mo. Ann. Stat. § 210.110(1)) "Emotional abuse" is not further defined in the statute.

Leaving the definition to professionals is not inappropriate.

We consider these statutes to meet CAPTA requirements as much as for what they do not say as for what is said. The statutes at least clearly include emotional abuse within the parameters of their reporting laws. Since no further definition is provided by the legislature, the enactment in each state of policy and guidelines will flesh out the meaning of emotional abuse. Leaving the definition to professionals is not inappropriate. They will be the ones setting the standards for training mandatory reporters, and their expertise can be brought to bear on the subject. As we shall see in the next chapter, many CPS agencies faced with just this situation create very thorough guidelines delineating what is to be reported and investigated for emotional abuse.

States that include emotional abuse (however referenced) in their statute without further defining the term are: Alabama, Connecticut,

Delaware, District of Columbia, Indiana, Kansas, Louisiana, Massachusetts, Michigan, Mississippi, Missouri, Nebraska, New Mexico, North Dakota, Ohio, Oklahoma, Utah and Virginia.

Outside of the states using model definitional language and those states using none, three states have created their own distinct language for defining emotional abuse. New Hampshire defines an "abused child" as one who has been "psychologically injured so that said child exhibits symptoms of emotional problems generally recognized to result from consistent mistreatment or neglect." N.H. Rev. Stat. Ann. §169-C:3.II.(c)

New Jersey, in its abuse definitions, includes the following:

> [A] child whose physical, mental, or emotional condition has been impaired or is in imminent danger of becoming impaired as the result of the failure of his parent or guardian, or such other person having his custody and control, to exercise a minimum degree of care (1) in supplying the child with adequate food, clothing, shelter, education, medical or surgical care though financially able to do so or though offered financial or other reasonable means to do so, or (2) In providing the child with proper supervision or guardianship, by unreasonably inflicting or allowing to be inflicted harm, or substantial risk thereof, including the infliction of excessive corporal punishment or using excessive physical restraint under circumstances which do not indicate that the child's behavior is harmful to himself, others or property; or by any other act of a similarly serious nature requiring the aid of the court. N.J. Stat. Ann. § 9:6-8.9.(d)

Finally, Rhode Island defines abuse to include the threat of harm to a child when a caretaker "creates or allows to be created a substantial risk of physical or mental injury to the child..." R.I. Gen. Laws §40-11-2.(1)(ii) "Mental injury" is then defined as,

> A state of substantially diminished psychological or intellectual functioning in relation to, but not limited to, such factors as: failure to thrive, ability to think or reason, control of aggressive or self-destructive impulses; acting-out or misbehavior; including incorrigibility, ungovernability, or habitual truancy; provided, however, that the injury must be clearly attributable to the unwillingness or inability of the parent or other person responsible for the child's welfare to exercise a minimum degree of care toward the child. § 40-11-2.(8).

One state has chosen to use some of the model language along with its own definition of emotional abuse. In Wisconsin, "emotional damage" is defined as:

> harm to a child's psychological or intellectual functioning. "Emotional damage" shall be evidenced by one or more of the following characteristics exhibited to a severe degree: anxiety; depression; withdrawal; outward aggressive behavior; or a substantial and observable change in behavior, emotional response or cognition that is not within the normal range for the child's age and stage of development. Wis. Stat. Ann. § 48.02(5j)

The only question about this definition is that it talks in terms of "severe" damage, whereas CAPTA addresses "serious" emotional harm. A legal argument could be made that "severe" requires a higher level of harm than would be necessary for "serious" damage. Hopefully, the last part of the statute, which speaks in terms of a "substantial and observable change in behavior...", would permit a professional to provide a diagnosis which was intended to be covered by the federal statute.

Finally, several states have gone the route of enacting statutory definitions that set out the types of behaviors necessary to meet the criteria for emotional damage or injury. For example, Arizona defines emotional abuse as:

> the infliction of or allowing an other person to cause serious emotional damage as evidenced by severe anxiety, depression, withdrawal or untoward aggressive behavior and which emotional damage is diagnosed by a medical doctor or psychologist and which is caused by the acts or omissions of an individual having care, custody and control of a child. Ariz. Rev. Stat. Ann. §8-201.2)

North Carolina has similar limitations, defining "serious emotional damage" as "severe anxiety, depression, withdrawal, or aggressive behavior toward himself or others." N.C. Gen. Stat. §7B-101(1)e

From a legal standpoint, these definitions meet the CAPTA standards of addressing serious emotional harm by looking at its impact upon a child whether it was caused by an act or omission of a caretaker. However, from a practice view, the fact that the legislature has specifically defined what behaviors will constitute emotional damage could limit the intervention in a given situation. While "anxiety, depression, withdrawal or untoward aggressive behavior" cover many of the symptoms of emotional abuse, the list is not necessarily inclusive of what a professional might determine to be exhibited in a child who suffers emotional damage. The point here is that, having required that a health professional diagnose the emotional injury, why not allow the evaluation and determination without placing limits on the behaviors that must be exhibited? This is especially true in light of on-going research that analyzes and interprets the brain, trauma, and emotional development. Our vocabulary has completely changed in the last ten years in this area as we are learning more each day.

From a practical standpoint, the professionals who analyze the case probably will not be stymied in acting on behalf of the child because of the statutory limits. From a legal standpoint, it is never particularly useful to have statutory language that could hinder rather than assist in carrying out what is the clear intent of the legislature—to protect a child from serious emotional abuse.

Like Arizona and North Carolina, Pennsylvania defines "serious mental injury" as a psychological condition that "renders a child chronically and severely anxious, agitated, depressed, socially withdrawn, psychotic or in reasonable fear that the child's life or safety is threatened." Pennsylvania avoids the problems of those states by adding an open standard defining the injury as a condition that "seriously interferes with a child's ability to accomplish age-appropriate development and social tasks." [23 Pa. Cons. Stat. Ann. §6303(A)]

Out of the state laws dealing with emotional abuse, the best definition is that found in the model language. The benefit of this particular language is that it generally defines the damage that can arise from emotional abuse and neglect and then leaves it to the professionals to appropriately diagnose a particular child. This type of abuse clearly needs to be left in the hands of professionals applying an appropriate diagnostic standard. Statutes that restrict the particular symptoms and behaviors that will trigger intervention potentially acknowledge the problem of emotional abuse, but restrict the actions of caseworkers in investigating and addressing the problem. Such restrictions can provide a rationale for non-intervention or justify a parent's lack of cooperation. These outcomes could be avoided with appropriate input and direction from professionals during the legislative process.

Statutes Not Conforming to CAPTA Requirements

All of the states discussed above have enacted legislation that, arguably, is adequate to meet the minimum standards required by CAPTA. However, there are several states where the statutory language does not exist or where it actually conflicts with the basic intent of the federal requirements.

• • • • • •

States Without Emotional Abuse Provisions in Their Reporting Statutes

The National Center on Child Abuse and Neglect (NCCAN), which tracks statutory provisions in all states relating to child abuse and neglect statutes, mandatory reporting requirements and criminal provisions relating to child abuse and neglect, presently identifies three states as failing to have reporting provisions relating to emotional abuse in their child abuse and neglect laws. Those states are California, Georgia and Washington.

California has taken the unusual step of including its child abuse and neglect statutes within its penal code. All other states include some offenses against children in its penal code (which would expose the perpetrator to criminal penalties including fines and imprisonment), but otherwise place the mandatory reporting laws relating to child abuse and neglect outside of the criminal section, in a place that will not entail criminal punishment, but does involve the public in oversight, and possible eventual dissolution, of the family unit. Even within the penal code, California defines abuse only as physical or sexual. [Cal. Penal Code § 11165.6] The sole reference to mental suffering comes in a curious section regarding out-of-home care. Abuse of a child in out-of-home care includes physical, sexual and "willful cruelty or unjustifiable punishment of a child." This last term is defined as a custodian who willfully causes or permits a child to suffer, among other things, "mental suffering." [Cal. Penal Code § 11165.3] The reporting requirements, based upon these abuse definitions, are located in the Penal Code in § 11166(a).

Apart from the abuse and neglect and reporting provisions of the California law, there is another, entirely different, section of California Code dealing with the authority of the juvenile court to find a child "dependent." Contained in the Welfare and Institutions Code, the provisions provide that a child can be brought within the jurisdiction of the juvenile court if a child has suffered or there is a substantial risk that the child will suffer (among other situations outlined in the section), physical harm, emotional damage or sexual abuse. With regard to the emotional component, that statute describes the basis for intervention as follows:

> The child is suffering serious emotional damage, or is at substantial risk of suffering serious emotional

> damage, evidenced by severe anxiety, depression, withdrawal, or untoward aggressive behavior toward self or others, as a result of the conduct of the parent or guardian or who has no parent or guardian capable of providing appropriate care. No child shall be found to be person described by this subdivision if the willful failure of the parent or guardian to provide adequate mental health treatment is based on a sincerely held religious belief and if a less intrusive judicial intervention is available. Cal. Wel. & Inst. Code § 300(c).

Since the issue of emotional maltreatment is scattered among several statutory locations, the ability to address the problem is certainly diffused and clouded. Seasoned CPS workers and supervisors may be able to navigate the process. However, emotional maltreatment cannot receive the attention it requires with such a fractured approach, especially since the purview of the juvenile court differs from that of the mandatory reporters. In other words, CPS can investigate and the juvenile court can act upon complaints of serious emotional damage, but the community and the mandated reporters are not required to be attentive to the problem. Our guess is that emotional abuse and neglect concerns become secondary evaluations after a physical or sexual abuse allegation brings a particular child to the attention to CPS.

In Georgia, Ga. Code Ann. §19-7-5 (b) defines child abuse for reporting purposes only in terms of physical and sexual abuse. On the other hand, § 15-11-94 provides for termination of parental rights upon a finding that a child is deprived and the deprivation will cause "serious physical, mental, emotional, or moral harm to the child." §15-11-94(b)(4)(A)(iv) However, looking at the effects of emotional and mental harm only within the context of parental termination is not enough. Emotional abuse cases need to be addressed far in advance of the circumstances that might lead to a termination proceeding. Interestingly, Georgia has enacted a criminal offense of "cruelty to children in the first degree" for a person who maliciously causes a child "cruel or excessive physical or mental pain." §16-5-70(b)

Despite this deficiency, Georgia's continuing legal education for superior and juvenile court judges has recently included training on the definitions, effects, and seriousness of emotional maltreatment.

The third state that does not include emotional abuse in its statute is Washington. Abuse and neglect are defined only as physical and sexual injury and negligent treatment. Wash. Rev. Code Ann. §26.44.020(12). Negligent treatment is defined as a serious disregard of clear and present dangers to a child's health, welfare and safety. "Severe abuse" is defined in §26.44.030(1)(c) as specific acts that result in severe physical trauma or sexual abuse or several acts resulting in serious physical injuries. There is no mention at all of emotional abuse. Child welfare workers would contend they evaluate emotional within the context of physical and sexual abuse cases, but they have no mandate at all to investigate a case that would be considered purely an emotional injury case. As long as there were no marks on a child who was being severely isolated or humiliated, for example, the State of Washington would not have authority to intervene. Washington also has no criminal provisions relating to emotional abuse.

• • • • • •

STATUTES REQUIRING AN INTENTIONAL ACT BY CARETAKER

Several states couch their abuse statutes in terms requiring a finding that the caretaker knowingly or intentionally inflicted an emotional or mental injury. This statutory language is in violation of the CAPTA focus on the impact of the actions on the child, not on the caretaker's intent. The language would mean a parent or custodian who engages in behavior that severely isolates, belittles or rejects a child, *but says he didn't know it would damage the child emotionally, could not be found to have abused the child.*

West Virginia defines an abused child as one whose health or welfare is harmed or threatened by a parent or custodian "who knowingly or intentionally inflicts, attempts to inflict or knowingly allows another person to inflict, physical injury or mental or emotional injury..." W.Va.Code Ann. §49-1-3(a)(1) It is one thing to be able to demonstrate a parent must have known he was inflicting a physical injury because of the physical damage. It is quite another to be required to prove the caretaker knew or intended to inflict an emotional injury.

Similarly, Minnesota defines "emotional maltreatment" as the "consistent, deliberate infliction of mental harm on a child." Minn. Stat. Ann. §260C.0007 Subd. 15 Vermont defines that same term as "a pattern of malicious behavior which results in impaired psychological growth, and development." Vt. Stat. Ann. tit. 33, §4912(7) To a lawyer, use of the terms "deliberate" and "malicious" traditionally involve proving an element of knowing and intentional behavior. Oregon defines abuse to include causing mental injury to a child, *but* requires substantial impairment to the child's psychological ability to function be caused "by cruelty to the child." Or. Rev. Stat. Ann. § 419B.005(1)(a)(A) Once again, in the law, cruelty involves a conscious and intentional act designed to cause injury.

Will there ever be a case where a caretaker admits he deliberately set out to damage a child psychologically?

By requiring proof that a caretaker intentionally and knowingly acted to cause an emotional injury, caseworkers in these states would be hamstrung in their efforts to combat serious and substantial cases of emotional abuse. Will there ever be a case where a caretaker admits he deliberately set out to damage a child psychologically? Without such an acknowledgment, evidence adequate to lead to a *permissible inference* that the parent knew the damaging effect of his actions and intended the injury would have to be brought before a court. Such evidence would be very difficult to acquire and prove and, for all practical purposes, would mean that a case based upon emotional abuse could not be successfully prosecuted in any of these states.

These four states have placed emotional abuse in their statute but, because of the way it has been defined, have removed it from any practical application except in the neglect or omission side of the equation. In other words, a caseworker could find a substantiated case of emotional neglect in a caretaker who has emotionally or mentally damaged a child by failing to do certain things, but could not substantiate a case where a parent's actions emotionally harmed a child. By requiring that the court look at the actions of the parent instead of evaluating harm done to a child, these statutes do not meet the CAPTA minimal requirements.

• • • • • •

Statutes Requiring Physical Injury for Emotional Abuse

In Illinois, the statute references "impairment of emotional health," but only within the context of physical injury. Let the language of the statute speak for itself. An abused child is one whose caretaker:

> Inflicts, causes to be inflicted, or allows to be inflicted upon such child *physical injury,* by other than accidental means, which causes death, disfigurement, impairment of physical or *emotional health,* or loss or impairment of any bodily function;
>
> Creates a substantial risk of *physical injury* to such child by other than accidental means which would be likely to cause death, disfigurement, impairment of physical or *emotional health,* or loss of impairment of bodily function. 325 Ill. Comp. Stat. Ann. 5/3 (emphasis supplied)

This unusual language allows a caseworker to evaluate emotional damage only when a physical injury or risk of physical injury exists. In addition, emotional injury is barely addressed in the neglect statute, which speaks of mental impairment only when a child is not receiving proper nourishment or medically indicated treatment. On the basis of the statutory definition, Illinois does not include within its mandatory reporting laws any requirement relating solely to emotional harm to a child.

This same language is found in the New York definition of an abused child. N.Y. Family Court Act § 1012(e)(i) and (ii) However, keep an eye out for how a New York court creatively managed to get around the requirement of a physical injury in an emotional abuse case. In a case that will be analyzed more extensively later, the court in *Matter of Shane T.*, 453 N.Y.S.2d 590 (N.Y. Fam. Ct. 1982) found that a stomach ache triggered by verbal emotional abuse was adequate as a "physical injury" to pull the emotional maltreatment within the protection of the statute.

• • • • • •

Statute Requiring Sexual Abuse for Emotional Injury

Idaho stands alone among the states that reference "mental injury" by including it only within the context of sexual abuse. The term is defined appropriately (substantial impairment in the psychological ability of a child to function within a normal range of performance), but the only reference to such abuse is found in the following paragraph of the section setting out the abuse standard for mandatory reporting. Idaho Code §16-1602 (a)(2) states that a child has been abused when he has been a victim of:

> Sexual conduct, including rape, molestation, incest, prostitution, obscene or pornographic photographing, filming or depiction for commercial purposes, or *other similar forms of sexual exploitation harming or threatening the child's health or welfare or mental injury to the child.* (Emphasis added)

The statute is awkward grammatically, but there is no doubt that mental injury is the subject of mandatory reporting only when it occurs in the context of a child being a victim of sexual abuse. Nowhere in the Idaho statute does mental injury stand on its own with regard to being a basis upon which abuse and/or neglect can be found.

On the other hand, the Idaho legislature has provided for taking a child into custody "where the child is endangered in his surroundings and prompt removal is necessary to prevent serious physical or mental injury to the child." §16-1612(a)(1) Seemingly, as with the case in California, this statute provides a backdoor to investigating a mental injury to a child. No mandatory reporter is required to report emotional abuse and neglect, but CPS can investigate it and courts can protect children from it. Again, the unfortunate aspect of this statute (other than it violates the federal requirements) is that it takes community response out of the equation. By statute, emotional abuse and neglect can only be an add-on to an investigation triggered by a report of physical or sexual abuse.

• • • • • •

By our count, the mandatory reporting requirements contained in the child abuse and neglect statutes of ten states do not meet the minimum standards of CAPTA. Statutes, of course, are subject to amendment, clarification, and complete change each legislative session. The lack of organization, consistency, and overall compliance to CAPTA guidelines that we see throughout the states may reflect the evolving understanding of this issue as well as the occurrence of specific "high profile" cases within a state that can often provoke changes.

In the best of all possible worlds, as with the Uniform Commercial Code and other broadly accepted model statutes, model language would be crafted and enacted across this country that would encompass not only appropriate language for emotional abuse and neglect, but all areas of child abuse and neglect. All those working on behalf of children across this country would benefit from applying similar standards and definitions. These standards would reflect a community conscience and recognition of the crucial need to protect children from the destruction of all types of child abuse and neglect.

The goal of the CPS worker is to determine whether that minimal level is being provided, and, if not, to take steps to see that it is.

Chapter Seven

CPS and the Investigation of Emotional Maltreatment

The fact that the scars of emotional maltreatment are invisible makes it easy to ignore. Compared to the damage of emotional abuse and neglect, it is relatively easy to identify marks, bruises, broken bones, sexual intercourse, oral sex and other assaults upon children that we classify as abusive. When a CPS worker responds to reports of physical and sexual abuse, for example, he or she will open the case, provide services, refer to community resources, and provide on-going supervision, regardless of whether a parent intended to cause damage. If the parent doesn't see the harm in his or her behavior or treatment of the child or refuses services, this does not affect the worker's need to provide protective supervision. If necessary, CPS will ask the court to mandate protective services or protective supervision, especially if the parent resists intervention. Regardless, the CPS agency proceeds to deliver remedial services, and this is generally referred to as "treatment."

This approach to investigation and response by child welfare services is based on the belief that there are societal understandings and expectations, founded on "best practice," i.e. research, history, casework and understanding of child development, that provide at least a minimal level of parental care necessary to ensure the healthy development of a child. The goal of the CPS worker is to determine whether that minimal level is being provided, and, if not, to take steps to see that it is. The intent of the parent may, of course, expedite change if the parent is accepting of help and support. However, if the parent does not see the harm of his or her actions and resists change, then CPS will respond accordingly to see that the child is protected.

Overview

We have previously referenced the fact that victims of emotional maltreatment are seriously underserved by the CPS system. There are probably various explanations for this lack of attention to emotional abuse and neglect. First, because there are no physical scars, there is a perception that this type of abuse is difficult to substantiate, and that it would be expensive to obtain the expert testimony necessary for an analysis and diagnosis. Second, many CPS agencies are directed, because of the need to allocate scarce dollars, to address only cases where a child is in "imminent" danger. There is a feeling that emotional maltreatment rarely falls within this context. Third, because emotional maltreatment has been the last of the abusive behaviors to be included in the reporting statutes, CPS agencies have yet to expand their attention to this type of abuse. Policy guidelines on the subject and training on recognizing it have not caught up with the statutory mandate. Finally, CPS professionals have been uncertain what creates the basis for intervention, e.g., the parent's intentions to cause harm with regard to his/her behaviors or the damage to the child.

...because emotional maltreatment has been the last of the abusive behaviors to be included in the reporting statutes, CPS agencies have yet to expand their attention to this type of abuse.

CPS is not the scapegoat in this scenario. Its attention to emotional abuse merely reflects the public's general lack of understanding about the devastating impact emotional abuse and neglect has on the development of a child. Lack of focus on emotional maltreatment is merely a reflection of a deficit in the public's knowledge about what a child needs in order to grow and develop normally. Society as a whole has not demanded that action be taken with regard to the emotional maltreatment of children.

> Perhaps one way to get a grip on CPS concerns is to compare where we are now in dealing with emotional abuse and neglect in the context of our history of dealing with sexual abuse.

Perhaps one way to get a grip on CPS concerns is to compare where we are now in dealing with emotional abuse and neglect in the context of our history of dealing with sexual abuse. Sexual abuse was rarely within the public's perception until the middle 1970's when federal requirements forced the establishment of child abuse statutes that created a mandatory reporting system and set up central registries for abuse reports. Over the next years, the public was educated to the devastation wrought upon a child who has been sexually abused. CPS now vigorously pursues such cases even though they require expert testimony to substantiate the abuse and do not truly fall into an "imminent" danger category in the way that physical abuse cases will. The child is not in "imminent" danger to his/her life, but there is, nevertheless, an acknowledgment by society that it is unacceptable for a child to have to endure such abuse.

Because the community came to understand the negative impact of sexual abuse on the healthy development of children, resources have been allocated and a process of dealing with perpetrators has been instituted in every state. The child advocacy center initiative has helped to establish a central venue in communities to holistically address all aspects of investigation, prosecution, and treatment in sexual abuse cases. Although the impetus for the child advocacy centers originated out of law enforcement (and specifically a former district attorney and now member of the United States House of Representatives, Robert E. "Bud" Cramer, of Huntsville, Alabama), CPS is now a willing partner in these efforts.

Therefore, sexual abuse marched past concerns about paying for expertise and whether a child is in "imminent" danger because the community became active and demanded that children be protected. CPS stepped up and educated itself and its mandatory reporters on the different kinds and signs of sexual abuse.

> We would argue that the cost of dealing with an emotional abuse case and the devastation to a child are no different than those implicated in a sexual abuse case.

We would argue that the cost of dealing with an emotional abuse case and the devastation to a child are no different than those implicated in a sexual abuse case. To make changes in addressing the needs of emotional maltreated children, however, we need to move forward within the CPS system with education and understanding of emotional maltreatment. Since CPS is the central point for collecting information on abuse allegations and frequently shapes the training given to mandatory reporters, the policies enacted by CPS to provide guidelines for its workers on emotional maltreatment must reflect current best practice as well as understanding of what emotional maltreatment is and its impact on children.

With regard to the remaining concern, i.e. whether parental intent or damage to a child will trigger intervention, the CAPTA standard clarifies that the *effect* of a caretaker's actions on a particular child and *not* whether that person *intended* to emotionally abuse or neglect the child must be the focus of CPS and of those who report incidents to the CPS system.

With emotional abuse and neglect, the intent to injure may be absent, yet intervention is required in order to protect the child. We have precedents in law and policy. Although a parent may not intend to hurt his child by not seeking medical attention or failing to provide adequate clothing or shelter, society will not tolerate these neglectful behaviors. A parent may not intend to hurt a three-month-old baby by shaking him to stop his crying, but when we find evidence of this, we are quick to act. Feeling a responsibility to ensure the safety and well being of every child, we have a history of acting on behalf of the child even when the intent to harm is absent. Intent really has importance only to evaluate the level of parental motivation, their understanding of child development and potential for change. It should not determine whether intervention is necessary.

> Intent … should not determine whether intervention is necessary.

There frequently are circumstances where parents do not have an understanding about behaviors that emotionally damage their children. Arguably, parents only rarely "intend" to cause such injury to their child. There was a time in the investigation of cases of physical abuse and sexual abuse that the same thing might have been said. It was unusual thirty years ago for the public to intervene when a parent slapped a child in public. There was a time when the public rarely inquired about what went on in the bedrooms of children. Now we feel that a parent is usually aware that society perceives such behavior to be wrong. We see parents hide physical or sexual abuse—certainly a testimony to the state of mind of the parent. This attempt to hide reflects at least a minimal understanding on the part of the abusing parent. We are at the point of beginning to establish a community standard for disapproving parental behaviors that are emotionally neglectful and abusive. As this understanding grows, we will someday feel more certain that a parent "intended" to cause harm with his words and destructive behaviors. In the meantime, we need CPS to focus on the welfare of the child.

Policy Guidelines for Emotional Maltreatment

The basis for an investigation of emotional maltreatment by CPS is the reporting statute in each state that defines that term. We have taken a look at those definitions. For those states requiring the reporting of incidents of mental or emotional abuse or neglect without defining those terms, child protective agencies are left to define the term through the implementation of policy. Policy is not state law. Policy is a set of guidelines that flush out how certain laws will be implemented by those mandated to enforce them. If a state does not define emotional abuse in its abuse and neglect statute, policy will be enacted to provide assistance to child welfare workers and other mandated reporters to clarify the actual scope of the statute.

The Family Independence Agency of Michigan specifically acknowledged this use of policy in its *Services Manual* for its Protective Services workers. In setting out the operational definitions for its child abuse and neglect investigations, the policy noted:

> The legal definitions for child abuse, child neglect, and child sexual abuse ... are narrowly defined based on the language of [the statute]. The following definitions are broader in scope and intended to better define child abuse, child neglect, and child sexual abuse for the purpose of giving better direction in the decision making process for intake and assignment of a complaint for investigation.

...policy itself will always be a shifting, changing body of language and priorities that can be effectively changed if errors or deficiencies are found within it.

The further point about policy, of course, is that nothing about it is carved in stone. Since it has been written and implemented by a governmental agency, it can be changed, updated, corrected or further defined by that same agency. Most states have a process for publication and comment about changes to and the enactment of policy, but policy itself will always be a shifting, changing body of language and priorities that can be effectively changed if errors or deficiencies are found within it.

Even in those states whose statues carry the more extensive definition of emotional abuse, policy is used to provide assistance to departments as to how such abuse is to be investigated and evaluated. Maryland's statute, for example, defines abuse as "the physical or mental injury of a child ... that indicate the child's health or welfare is harmed or at substantial risk of being harmed" and further defines "mental injury" as "the observable, identifiable, and substantial impairment of a child's mental or psychological ability to function." Md. Code Ann. Fam. Law. § 5-701(b)(1) and (q) Maryland's *policy* enlarges upon these definitions by providing the framework for an investigation of a case involving mental injury, including the assessment by two licensed professionals (physician, psychologist, or social worker, including a department worker) of whether a mental injury exists. The assessment is specifically required through the policy guidelines to:

Even in those states whose statues carry the more extensive definition of emotional abuse, policy is used to provide assistance to departments as to how such abuse is to be investigated and evaluated.

- Determine whether the child has sustained a mental injury.
- Describe the "observable, identifiable, and substantial impairment" of the child's ability to function.
- If applicable, determine the act or omission believed to have caused the mental injury.

Maryland's guidelines go on to clarify that mental injury will be categorized either as "abuse" if the injury is caused by an act to a child or as "neglect" if the injury is caused by an "omission or failure to act on behalf of the child." Therefore, through its statute and the additional framework set out in its guidelines, Maryland has fulfilled the CAPTA requirements of addressing substantial emotional harm, whether by acts or failures to act, which impacts a child's psychological ability to function.

Some state policy guidelines appear to walk a fine line between statutory language that inappropriately defines emotional abuse or mental injury and a professional's understanding of the implications of this type of abuse.

Some state policy guidelines appear to walk a fine line between statutory language that inappropriately defines emotional abuse or mental injury and a professional's understanding of the implications of this type of abuse. For example, even though the Illinois statute inappropriately defines impairment to "emotional health" only when it results from a physical injury, the Illinois Department of Children and Family Services appropriately defines "mental injury" in its Administrative Rules as "injury to the intellectual, emotional or psychological development of a child as evidenced by observable and substantial impairment in the child's ability to function within a normal range of performance and behavior, with due regard to his or her culture." The Rules go on, unfortunately, to define mental injury due to "abuse" as arising only from a non-accidental physical injury (the statutory language) but then seems to open up the definition by also including "threat of injury." The real area where the Department appears to go beyond the statutory language is defining mental injury as arising from "neglect" when a caretaker disregards his/her responsibilities for providing the necessary care for a child's well being.

This uncertainty in meaning and approach found in the Illinois policy reflects the overall problem that occurs when the professional community runs up against statutory language that violates best practice and understanding of the effects of emotional maltreatment. Although this policy cannot quite get away from the "physical injury" part of the Illinois statute, there is an effort made to soften the position by speaking to "necessary care for the child's well being."

The Pennsylvania guidelines clarify otherwise confusing statutory language. The statute defines child abuse as "an act or failure to act by a perpetrator which causes nonaccidental serious mental injury." The guidelines help us understand what is meant by a "nonaccidental mental injury" by defining child abuse as a mental injury "which is not explained by the available medical history as being accidental." That helps to clear up confusion that would otherwise lead one to the conclusion that Pennsylvania defined mental injury as occurring only when intentionally caused by a caretaker.

In North Carolina, even though the statute narrowly defines the term "serious emotional damage" as evidenced by a child's "severe anxiety, depression, withdrawal or aggressive behavior toward himself or others," the Department of Human Resources, Division of Social Services, has set in place a "Child Mental Health Evaluation Program," which creates a framework to assess whether a child is suffering from emotional abuse. The professionals carrying out the evaluation must be licensed psychiatrists or psychologists and are given a mandate to thoroughly evaluate a child, his symptoms of emotional disorder and family dysfunction. There clearly are no limits placed upon what symptoms of emotional damage will be evaluated in doing a complete mental health evaluation. As professionals, the Department would know the specific symptoms set out in statute do not adequately cover the gamut of symptoms related to serious emotional damage.

The actual terms of the North Carolina statute, "severe anxiety, depression, withdrawal or aggressive behavior toward himself and others," although statutorily narrow, will virtually include any behavior the child may exhibit that is deemed to be abnormal and a barrier to his healthy emotional development. In the hands of the professionals responsible for the "Child Mental Health Evaluation Program, the wording of this statue can be applied very effectively.

Missouri's statute defines "abuse" as "emotional abuse inflicted on a child other than by accidental means by those responsible for the child's care custody, and control." The definition seems to require some intentional act on the part of the caretaker. However, child welfare policy defines "emotional maltreatment" as "a passive or active patterned non-nurturing behavior by a parent or caretaker that negatively affects and/or handicaps a child emotionally, psychologically, physically, intellectually, socially, and/or developmentally." This policy moves past intent to focus on outcome regardless of the state of mind of the adult.

Missouri policy includes descriptions of indicators of emotional maltreatment to be used in assessment to include not only child behavioral indicators, but also a child's physical indicators and family/parental characteristics and behavioral indicators. A Missouri children's services worker is to evaluate parental behaviors such as scapegoating, extremely inappropriate expectations, rejection, ignoring, withholding love, marital conflict, and lack of understanding of appropriate child-rearing practices. The investigator is to assess a child's failure to thrive, stress-related physical symptoms, blank expression, lags in physical and intellectual development as well as the child's maladaptive behaviors such as self-destructive tendencies, behavior extremes, inappropriately adult or infantile and neurotic problems such as depression and/or anxiety. Missouri's investigation manual, designed to provide professional guidelines and standards, makes an obvious effort to fill in the gaps left by the statutory definition.

Oklahoma is also very thorough in providing guidance with regard to the parental behaviors to be analyzed in an evaluation of mental injury. The statute merely defines mental injury in an abuse context as nonaccidental harm or threatened harm to a child's health or safety. The child protective services manual, however, defines "mental injury" as "an injury to the child's intellectual or psychological capacity as evidenced by observable and substantial impairment in the child's ability to function within his/her normal range of performance and behavior with due regard to the child's culture." The definition includes both abuse and neglect. The manual then lists a series of behaviors that "could indicate mental injury if it is established that the situation is observable, substantial and a pattern." Such behaviors include:

- acts directed at the child that degrade and/or belittle;
- threatening extreme or vague but sinister punishments;
- setting unrealistic expectations-ignoring or being psychologically unavailable to the child;
- failing to respond to or show affection to the child;
- showing little or no attachment to child and failing to nurture the child;
- making inappropriate demands of the child that are beyond the child's capabilities;
- confusing the child's sexual identity; and/or
- exposing the child to maladaptive and harmful influences-repeatedly ridicules the child.

In Oklahoma, the protocol for confirming a mental injury requires the following:

- Identification of an observable and substantial impairment of his/her intellectual and/or emotional functioning;
- Demonstration of a pattern of emotional abusive or neglectful behavior by the caretaker;
- A professional opinion that the caretaker's behavior causes the impairment in the child's intellectual or emotional impairment; and
- Documentation of the above by statements of the child and of the caretaker; evidence from others

> familiar with the family and the caseworker's observation and assessment of the child's behavior and demeanor.

A contrast to the thorough job done in the Oklahoma child protective services manual is that of Nebraska. The Nebraska statute defines abuse and neglect as "knowingly, intentionally, or negligently causing or permitting a minor child" to be placed "in a situation that endangers his or her life or physical or mental health." Nebraska also includes being "cruelly confined or cruelly punished" in its abuse and neglect statute, which arguably could have an emotional abuse component. Nebraska's Department of Social Services Manual defines child maltreatment as occurring when a child is "physically, emotionally, or sexually harmed so the child's emotional, cognitive, or physical development is or will be impaired, and the parent is unwilling or unable to protect the child." While this definition seemingly opens up the scope of emotional abuse that could be investigated by the department, the following specific definitions of emotional abuse and neglect are narrowly drawn. Emotional abuse is defined as:

> Information indicates continual scapegoating or rejection of a child by his/her parents, which result in psychopathological or disturbed behavior in the child which can be documented by a psychiatrist, psychologist or social worker.

Emotional neglect is defined as having occurred when:

> Information indicates that the child is suffering or has suffered severe negative emotional effects due to a parent's failure to provide opportunities for normal experience that produce feelings of being loved, wanted, secure and worthy. Lack of such opportunities may impair the child's ability to form healthy relationships with others. Examples include emotional deprivation, not providing mental health

services for a child when indicated or a child being shunned by peers due to lack of hygiene.

It is unfortunate that the Nebraska manual focuses only on such abusive behaviors as scapegoating and rejection, when the mental health community clearly understands that such abuse includes many, many more behaviors than those enumerated.

It is very important that the CPS system do a good job of providing best practice guidelines to its workers on emotional maltreatment. These guidelines become the basis for training on investigating abuse and neglect complaints and for educating mandated reporters. Of course, this education process cannot occur if policy has not been enacted to provide appropriate guidance to its workers, guidance that reflects a current understanding of the parental behaviors to be examined and the effect of those behaviors on children.

It is very important that the CPS system do a good job of providing best practice guidelines to its workers on emotional maltreatment.

The Court's Deference to Policy

Once guidelines on emotional maltreatment have been enacted through policy, the courts will pay attention because they recognize that people who have expertise in that particular field have promulgated the policies. The courts recognize the need for clarification of otherwise minimal statutory language so that those mandated to enforce the statute can appropriately carry out their obligations.

Let's take a look at a case where a Virginia appellate court confirmed the authority of CPS to define emotional maltreatment through policy and to implement an investigation based upon that policy. Since Virginia is one of the states that does not explicitly define emotional abuse and neglect, the deference to CPS is logical. This case not only defers to CPS for definition but also is very clear on the issue of intent, making it very helpful in crafting a practical approach to protecting children from emotional maltreatment.

As background for this discussion, Virginia Code § 63.1-248.2(A) defines an abused or neglected child as one:

> Whose parents or other person responsible for his care creates or inflicts, threatens to create or inflict, or allows to be created or inflicted upon such child a physical or mental injury by other than accidental means, or creates a substantial risk of death, disfigurement or impairment of bodily or mental functions...

Although no further definition is provided for "mental injury" or "impairment of ... mental functions," the Virginia Department of Social Services promulgated guidelines for those terms in its *Protective Services Manual*. That policy now states as follows:

> **Mental Abuse/Neglect** *(This category is often referred to an emotional abuse/neglect)*
>
> A pattern of acts or omissions by the caretaker which result in harm to a child's psychological or emotional health or development. The child demonstrates psychological or emotional dysfunction as a result of the caretaker's action/inaction. It is recommended that professional documentation be obtained to support the existence of such dysfunction. Such acts or omission may include:

- Caretaker behavior which is rejecting, intimidating, humiliating, ridiculing, chaotic, bizarre, violent, hostile or excessively guilt-producing, and which results in demonstrated dysfunction by the child.
- Caretaker actions/inactions such as: overprotection, ignoring, indifference, rigidity, apathy, chaotic lifestyle, or other behaviors related to the caretaker's own mental problems, and which results in demonstrated dysfunction by the child.

In *Jackson v. W.,* 14 Va.App. 391, 419 S.E.2d 385 (1992), the Washington County Department of Social Services (hereinafter "DSS") investigated a complaint concerning a father's alleged emotional abuse of his seven-year-old son. After an investigation, a DSS case worker determined that the emotional abuse was "founded," an action that placed the father's name on the Central Registry of the State of Virginia. The father exercised his right of appeal, but the local director of the DSS upheld the "founded" disposition. The father then appealed to the Commissioner of the Virginia Department of Social Services.

The record before the Commissioner contained the DSS investigation and reports, as well as notes from professionals who had worked with the child. The following behaviors by the father were determined to be inappropriate, "abnormal, humiliating and psychologically harmful" to the child: "forcing the child to take a bottle, vigorous scrubbing of the child's penile and anal areas during mutual showers, placing vaseline on the child's anal area, and cleaning the child's anal area after defecation." The father acknowledged the allegations but contended that they were for proper hygiene or "fantasy play" that did not damage the child. The hearing officer upheld the "founded" determination by the local DSS as " 'behaviors which are considered intimidating, humiliating ... or excessively guilt-producing' as specified in policy."

The father appealed that decision to the local circuit court and specifically challenged the policy guidelines. The circuit court agreed with the father and ruled that the Commissioner did not have authority to adopt the guidelines, that the guidelines were inconsistent with the abuse and neglect statute and were unconstitutionally vague. The Commissioner appealed this action to the Court of Appeals of Virginia.

The Virginia appellate court rejected all of the circuit court rulings and made the following rulings:

1. That the Commissioner by statute was authorized to enact rules to assist in implementing a statute. The court noted that the

Commissioner could not enact "regulations" but was empowered to administer all laws pertaining to the DSS and, accordingly, had the power to establish guidelines to assist the DSS to carry out its statutory mandate to protect children from abuse and neglect.

2. That, although policy guidelines are not binding on a court, policy has been implemented by people experienced in the field and a court will grant it deference and will look to it for guidance.
3. With regard to the father's contention that the policy did not conform to the abuse and neglect statute, the appellate court stated that it would give "great deference" to the agency's interpretation of the law it was mandated to enforce. Only if that interpretation were "arbitrary or capricious" would it be reversed.

The professionals agreed that the father may have not intended to inflict a mental injury, but the behavior had, nevertheless, caused significant emotional disturbance.

Also of interest in the court's decision, the father challenged the guidelines (and the circuit court had agreed with him), arguing that they "permitted a finding of mental abuse based solely upon the behavior of the parent or caretaker, even in the absence of any mental injury to the child." However, the appellate court disagreed with the father's contention that there had been no mental injury to his son by pointing out that there had been expert testimony in the case that the father's actions were embarrassing, abnormal, humiliating, and psychologically harmful to the child. The professionals agreed that the father may have not intended to inflict a mental injury, but the behavior had, nevertheless, caused significant emotional disturbance. The appellate court rejected the father's argument holding that "the statutory definitions of an abused or neglected child do not require proof of actual harm or impairment having been experienced by the child." The Court stated:

> The Commonwealth's policy is to protect abused children and to prevent further abuse of those children. *This policy would be meaningless if a child must suffer an actual injury from the behavior of his or her parent before receiving the Commonwealth's protection.* Neither the statute nor the guidelines impose such trauma upon a child. 419 S.E. 2d at 391. (Emphasis supplied)

Finally, the court rejected the father's contention that the terms "rejecting, intimidating, humiliating, ridiculing, chaotic, bizarre, violent, hostile, or excessively guilt-producing" were unconstitutionally vague and too open to interpretation. The appellate court noted that the guidelines were intended to interpret "mental injury" and were to assist caseworkers to identify abuse and neglect and described conduct which, "when measured by common practice and understanding," may be abusive.

It is time for CPS systems across the country to move forward in updating policy and training for mandatory reporters in the area of emotional maltreatment

The *Jackson* case demonstrates very clearly that CPS will be rewarded when it takes the time and trouble to thoughtfully enact policy guidelines for investigation that reflect the current professional understanding of emotional abuse and neglect. The court in *Jackson* gave substantial respect to CPS in regard to best practice, and at the same time, sent a message that the primary goal was to assure the health and welfare of the child. It is time for CPS systems across the country to move forward in updating policy and training for mandatory reporters in the area of emotional maltreatment so that the same emphasis that has been focused on physical and sexual abuse can be aimed at this devastating form of abuse and neglect.

It is certainly incumbent upon professionals to have accurate information regarding the law, policy, as well as the current judicial treatment of emotional maltreatment, if appropriate decisions are to be made as to which cases are brought to the attention of the court.

Chapter Eight

Courts Look at Emotional Maltreatment

Once the legislature has enacted statutes and agencies have implemented policy to interpret and explain those statutes, courts put "legs" on the statutes by applying them to cases brought before them. Usually, these cases are brought by a child welfare agency on behalf of a child to either remove a child from a parent's custody or to terminate parental rights. The courts will examine the evidence presented by the department to determine whether it rises to an appropriate level and whether it conforms to the statutory definitions applicable to the relief being sought.

In our efforts to bring only cases to the attention of the court that we feel we can "win" or gain our desired result, we try to predict how the court will react in advance of the petition. Since the CPS system must work within a judicial system that is normally geared to "winning" or "losing" a case, this prediction about what the judge will do can shape our practice and determine our plans for children, all perhaps while predicting an erroneous legal response. This "second guessing" of the court erodes the overall effectiveness of judges since there cannot be a ruling on a case that is never brought. Perhaps without meaning to do so, the CPS system has limited the opportunities for the court to consider new knowledge and research that could shape a more aggressive approach to protecting children from emotional maltreatment.

In addition, with the changing currents of thought and law involving children, it is impossible to know how the court will react. To predict can be not only unwise but can pose a serious threat for a child. Since dependency and termination of parental rights proceedings are generally unavailable for review except on the appellate level, gauging the response of the court to new information is difficult and misleading. Day-to-day cases brought to the lower court are considered in closed hearings, and the records are typically confidential. Only the findings in cases appealed to a higher court are available for public viewing. Therefore, it is virtually impossible to get an accurate "feel" for where a particular court stands today, or where it is moving on emerging issues. The informal discussions that occur within the CPS environment about the positions, philosophies, and attitudes of certain judges can jeopardize the opportunities that CPS has to bring the court along with new thought and research.

...review of appellate cases appears to demonstrate that courts are not at all antagonistic to dealing with emotional maltreatment issues.

However, review of appellate cases appears to demonstrate that courts are not at all antagonistic to dealing with emotional maltreatment issues. It is certainly incumbent upon professionals to have accurate information regarding the law, policy, as well as the current judicial treatment of emotional maltreatment, if appropriate decisions are to be made as to which cases are brought to the attention of the court.

Many times supervisors have argued with an attorney representing the CPS agency about whether a petition should be filed, a case "settled," or whether to move forward. The attorney, if untrained in family court law, finds it difficult to see child dependency outside the realm of civil litigation or criminal proceedings. However, the responsibility of the CPS department is to bring these cases to the attention of the court when the child is in danger, regardless of the circumstances. Failure to seek the assistance of the courts belittles the wisdom and responsibility of the court.

Evidentiary Standards in Investigation/Removal Versus Termination Cases

In order for the CPS system to respond appropriately to cases of emotional maltreatment, social workers, supervisors, and their attorneys must act to protect the child, always aware that the rules of evidence vary according to what is asked of the court as relief. The level of evidence necessary to, for example, find a child in need of assistance or services or in need of removal from a home is different from that required to terminate parental rights. The findings, which would be adequate for a finding of "founded" or "substantiated" in an abuse and neglect investigation and provide a basis for removal of a child from the house, may or may not be sufficient to terminate rights and allow adoption of a child. In addition, the statutory basis for investigating a complaint of abuse or neglect is frequently different from that which justifies a termination proceeding.

A "preponderance" standard is generally defined as merely needing to tip the scales from balanced to one favoring the position being taken by the department.

A parent's right to establish a home and raise a child is generally protected as an element of "liberty" found in both the Fifth and Fourteenth Amendments to the United States Constitution. Because a constitutional right is at stake, the standard that is applied in a termination proceeding is that of "clear and convincing evidence." Legally, this is a heightened evidentiary standard that is greater than the "preponderance of the evidence" which would be adequate for finding that a child is in need of services and/or a removal petition. A "preponderance" standard is generally defined as merely needing to tip the scales from balanced to one favoring the position being taken by the department. "Clear and convincing" requires a more rigorous evidentiary standard then merely tipping the scales, but does not rise to the level of "beyond a reasonable doubt," the requirement for conviction in a criminal case.

There appears to be one exception to the "clear and convincing" standard in termination cases. Where the parents are of Native American descent, the provisions of the Indian Child Welfare Act (ICWA), 25 United States Code, Section 1901 *et seq.*, come into play. Section 1912(f) of the ICWA provides that:

> No termination of parental rights may be ordered ... in the absence of a determination, supported by evidence *beyond a reasonable doubt,* including testimony of qualified expert witnesses, that the continued custody of the child by the parent or Indian custodian is likely to result in serious emotional or physical damage to the child. (Emphasis supplied).

As far as the authors can tell, the ICWA is the only exception to the "clear and convincing" standard for termination cases that otherwise exists in every state.

The Supreme Court of the United States settled the issue of what standard is to apply in a parental termination case in *Santosky v. Kramer,* 455 U.S. 745, 102 S.Ct. 1388, 71 L.Ed.2d (1982). In *Santosky,* the state of New York had established a "preponderance" standard in termination cases, a standard challenged by parents whose rights had been terminated. The Supreme Court determined that, because of the importance of the constitutional right involved, due process required the application of a "clear and convincing" standard, but rejected the argument that "beyond a reasonable doubt" should be required. With regard to its rejection of the criminal standard in parental termination cases, the Court stated:

> Like civil commitment hearings, termination proceedings often require the factfinder to evaluate medical and psychiatric testimony, and to decide issues difficult to prove to a level of absolute certainty, such as lack of parental motive, absence of affection between parent and child, and failure of parental foresight and progress. 455 U.S. at 769.

Even though parents have a constitutional right to raise children without undue interference, the Supreme Court has also recognized that this right is subordinated to a child's right to be protected in his health and safety. *See, Wisconsin v. Yoder,* 406 U.S. 205 (233-34), 92 S. Ct. 1526, 1542, 32 L.Ed.2d 15 (1971) (parents' constitutional rights may be overcome if health or safety of a child is in jeopardy); *Stankosky v. Kramer, supra*, 455 U.S. at 766 (states have a *parens patriae* interest "in preserving and promoting the welfare of the child.")

Following these Supreme Court decisions, state courts acknowledge that a parent has a constitutional right to raise his children, but that such rights are not without limit and must be viewed within the context of the best interests of the child. This position was stated succinctly in *State ex rel. J.L.V. v. State,* 958 P.2d 943 (Utah Ct. App. 1998) as follows:

> Like other cases affecting the custody of children, courts deciding abuse, neglect, and dependency cases are obligated to promote the best interests of the children involved. (citations omitted) The Legislature has determined ... that in cases involving a petition alleging the abuse, neglect, or dependency of a child, the parental presumption does not apply. In other words... the law does not presume that it is in a child's best interests to be in the custody of the child's parent when that parent has been found by clear and convincing evidence to have neglected or abused the child, or when the child is dependent. *Id.* at 948.

This determination of the court is especially important as the rhetoric has increased concerning "parental rights." Groups who support the rights of parents such as VOCAL (Victims of Child Abuse Legislation) have focused on this friction between the rights of parents and the rights of children. Parents can assert their rights by retaining an attorney, filing suit, or seeking to amend or set aside court orders. Children, when there is controversy between what the parent sees as appropriate care of the child and what is perceived by community standards or statutory mandates, are dependent on the action taken by advocates, the CPS system and the court to address their rights and concerns. The court becomes the place where everyone is allowed to voice his opinion, but the focus must always remain on determining the best interests of an, otherwise, voiceless child.

The different evidentiary standards to be applied at the investigation and termination phases of intervention are complicated because the language of the child abuse and neglect reporting statutes and the termination provisions rarely provide the same grounds for examining parental behaviors. Instead, the provisions are too often so dissimilar that the evidence that would trigger an investigation might not necessarily support a termination proceeding. For instance, as we have seen in Georgia, a complaint of emotional abuse would not trigger a CPS investigation but would be pertinent when it came time to terminate parental rights. What would make the most sense is if the two standards generally referenced the same prohibited acts with regard to child abuse and neglect. (Termination provisions normally contain grounds other than abuse, e.g. abandonment and long-term imprisonment.) Then, the reporting and investigation level would apply a preponderance of the evidence standard in determining whether a complaint is "founded." The evidentiary standard of proof would move to the higher level of "clear and convincing" if termination were based upon abuse and neglect allegations.

• • • • • •

The Courts and Abuse and Neglect Issues in General

Courts Will Interpret the Intent of the Legislature

The question of whether a child has been abused or neglected normally calls for application of the statutory definitions established by the legislature. As we have seen, much of the statutory language relating to abuse and neglect is drawn in very broad terms. What happens when appellate courts face what is considered a case of "first impression" i.e., one that raises a legal question never before considered in the state? In those cases, a court will normally attempt to determine "the intent of the legislature" when it enacted the legislation. The courts begin by reviewing any introductory language to the abuse and neglect sections where the overall purpose of the statute is stated. This will influence a court's determination whether a particular factual situation was to be impacted by the general language of the abuse or neglect legislation.

The courts begin by reviewing any introductory language to the abuse and neglect sections in which the overall purpose of the statute is stated.

As an example of a state's policy in enacting child protective provisions, the legislature of Maine stated its intent to provide a system to remove children from abusive situations and locate a permanent placement for them "recognizing that the health and safety of children must be of paramount concern and that the right to family integrity is limited by the right of children to be protected from abuse and neglect..." 22 M.R.S. § 4003. This clear statement of priorities gives guidance to CPS and the courts in analyzing factual situations in removal and termination proceedings.

In *State ex rel. C.J.K.*, 774 So. 2d 107 (La. 2000), the Supreme Court of Louisiana faced what was a novel question to them of whether a mother's rights should be terminated because she had repeatedly allowed her children to be exposed to their father's domestic violence. The Supreme Court observed the Louisiana legislature had expressed an intent that the termination provisions be construed liberally. 774 So.2d at 115. The Court also noted the legislature had "defined a 'neglected' child in broad terms precisely because foreseeing all the possible factual situations that may arise is impossible." *Id.* Noting that exposure to violence could result in severe psychological abuse, the Supreme Court applied legislative intent and approved the termination.

In *Matter of Shane T*, *supra*, a New York family court judge determined verbal abuse alone could be sufficient to terminate parental rights. The judge noted the legislature had established "procedures to help protect children from injury or mistreatment and to help safeguard their physical, mental and emotional well-being." After reviewing the evidence, the court stated:

> To constitute abuse, mere words are sufficient provided that their effect on the child falls within the language of the statute. To hold otherwise would constitute an unjustifiably narrow interpretation of the statute that would frustrate the legislature's intent. *Id.* at 593.

The Supreme Court of Montana in *In re C.A.R.*, 214 Mont. 174, 693 P.2d 1214 (Mont. 1984) examined an appeal from an order terminating parental rights. The Court began its consideration by reviewing the policy set forth by the Montana legislature to "insure that all youth are afforded an adequate physical and emotional environment to promote normal development...."

For those working on abuse and neglect cases where statutory language is drafted in broad terms, it never hurts to emphasize the "intent of the legislature" because normally there is a clear focus on protecting the well being of children. Providing evidence that fits within this language provides a sound basis for a good result with the appellate courts as they attempt to further that intent.

Courts Will Not Find Statutes to Be Unconstitutionally Vague

The same broad language that sets the courts to seek out the intention of the legislature can also lead to a challenge that the language is so vague that it violates the constitutional rights of those who have been found to have committed abuse or neglect. It is a basic tenet of constitutional law that a statute must be specific enough about the act that it seeks to regulate that someone who is prosecuted for violating the law would know that his actions fell within the parameters of the language. Given the general nature of abuse and neglect statutes, it is not unusual that they are challenged on this basis. Courts, however, have consistently turned back these challenges.

In *People v. D.A.K.*, 198 Colo. 11, 596 P.2d 747 (1979); appeal dismissed, 444 U.S. 987, 100 S.Ct. 515, 62 L.Ed.2d 416 (1979), the Supreme Court of Colorado was one of the first state appellate courts to hold that the general term "abuse" included emotional abuse. The Colorado statute at that time defined a neglected or dependent child as one whose parent had subjected him to "mistreatment or abuse." A mother who had been charged with abusing her child argued on appeal that this language was so "vague and uncertain that it fails to meet the constitutional requirements for statutory definiteness." 596 P.2d at 750. The Supreme Court disagreed, stating:

> An ordinarily responsible parent can understand what it means to "abuse" and "mistreat" a child. Fundamental fairness does not require a statute to enumerate in all-encompassing examples, or exactly described acts, precisely how poorly a parent can treat a child before risking loss of parental rights … . Furthermore, the statute is as explicit as could be in order to accomplish the purposes intended. (citation omitted) The protection of an abused or mistreated child is an area of legitimate legislative concern that does not lend itself to more precise definition. A legislature would find it extremely difficult, if not impossible, to write a statute more specific to accomplish the purposes of protecting the child's safety and welfare while still allowing the juvenile court reasonable flexibility in determining the best interests of the child and society in each case. *Id.* at 751.

A father challenged the Kansas statute defining a child in need of care who "has been physically, mentally or emotionally abused or neglected or sexually abused" as being unconstitutionally vague.

The Court of Appeals of Kansas in *In the Interest of Ra.R.*, 793 P.2d 767 (Kan. Ct. App. 1990) disagreed:

> We are convinced that a common-sense reading of [the statute] indicates that the statute sufficiently warns persons potentially subject to it. "Physical, mental or emotional abuse or neglect" ... covers a broad range of conduct and does not particularize all conduct that might fall within the reach of the statute. However, such specificity is not constitutionally required. (Citation omitted) Moreover, the terms used in the statute are not so vague that persons of common intelligence must guess at the meaning of the phrase "physical, mental or emotional abuse or neglect." The statute uses words of commonly understood meaning. 793 P.2d at 772.

Finally, in *Jackson v. W, supra*, a father challenged the "mental injury" policy guidelines enacted by the Department of Social Services, contending that they were unconstitutionally vague. The Court of Appeals of Virginia rejected this point. In researching case law in other states, the Court found that courts in Delaware, Michigan, Georgia, New Mexico, and North and South Dakota had reviewed similar language and had always upheld the statutes against a vagueness challenge.

It appears that the point is well settled that appellate courts will defer to juvenile courts hearing cases involving child and abuse and neglect. The lower courts are generally given wide discretion to weigh evidence and expert testimony in determining whether a particular set of circumstances come within the purview of the child abuse and neglect statutes. Phrases such as "fundamental fairness," "common sense reading" and "common intelligence" speak to the willingness of the court to accept what some may call "vague." There seems to be a general acceptance that dealing with family dynamics rarely involves issues that are black and white. Given how blurred and gray the evidence might be, deference will be paid to the decision of the fact finder who listened to and saw the participants in the courtroom.

Courts Will Find Statutes to Be Preventative in Nature

There is a clear thread running through the courts of many states that the abuse and neglect statutes are to be interpreted as preventative. In other words, the state should not sit around and wait for a child to be damaged before stepping in and dealing with a situation that is of obvious danger for the child. For example, in *E.J.R. v. Young (In re J.R.),* 162 Vt. 219, 646 A.2d 1284 (1994), the Supreme Court of Vermont rejected the parents' contention that their daughter was not a child in need of supervision (CHINS). The parents argued actual harm must have been inflicted before she could be removed from the home. The Court stated: "We further note that a neglect or dependency proceeding is preventative as well as remedial." 162 Vt. at 223, 646 A.2d at 1286.

In *Interest of Cheatwood*, 108 Idaho 218, 697 P.2d 1232 (Idaho Ct. App. 1985), a parent whose rights had been terminated for neglect argued that there had been no evidence presented that her neglect had caused "substantial harm" to her son. The appellate court stated "nothing in the statutory definition of 'neglect' suggests that a child must suffer demonstrable harm before the parent-child relationship can be terminated .... The termination statutes of this state exist not merely to alleviate harm but to prevent it." 108 Idaho at 220, 697 P.2d at 1234.

A father challenged a CHINS finding with regard to his four children in *Roark v. Roark,* 551 N.E.2d 865 (Ind. Ct. App. 1990), contending that the abuse and neglect statute required that the children must have sustained an injury due to his act or omission, and that none of the children had an injury when taken into custody. The appellate court held that "the CHINS statutes do not require that the courts and the Welfare Department wait until a tragedy occurs to intervene; a child is a Child in Need of Services when it is endangered by parental action or inaction." *Id.* at 872 (emphasis in original).

In *In Interest of N.H.*, 383 N.W.2d 570 (Iowa 1986), a mother had petitioned for the termination of the parental rights of her children's father. The petition had been denied by the juvenile court based upon a determination that the termination statute required that services had to offered to a parent before the abuse that was the basis for termination had occurred. The mother appealed. The Supreme Court of Iowa agreed with the mother that the juvenile court had misinterpreted the statute, stating that the lower court's construction "would require that a child be abused twice before parental rights could be terminated." *Id.* at 572. The Court said:

> It is our view that the current statutory termination provision applicable here .... are preventative as well as remedial. The provisions therefore mandate action to prevent probable harm to a child and do not require delay until after harm has occurred. *Ibid.* citing *In re Dameron,* 306 N.W..2d 743, 745 (Iowa 1981).

Finally, the Court stated: "We need not gamble with the child's welfare and future by subjecting the child to future abuse before a parental rights termination can take place." *Id.* at 573.

Montana's Supreme Court in *In* the *Matter of A.M.*, 304 Mont. 379, 22 P.3d 185 (2001), confirmed that the statutory language in the child abuse and neglect statute, which included "harm or threatened harm to a child's health or welfare by the acts or omissions of a person responsible for the child's welfare," meant that a child determined to be "in danger of being abused or neglected" could be considered in need of care "whether *actual* abuse or neglect occurred." 304 Mont. at 391, 22 P.3d at 194 (emphasis in original). The Court noted that *"threatened harm"* meant "a substantial risk of harm to the child's health or welfare" and could, as much as actual harm, form the basis for a determination that the child needed assistance.

These cases present a compelling argument for prevention efforts throughout the community. With the court using terms like *threatened harm, substantial risk,* and *in danger of being abused or neg-*

lected, we have a judicial mandate to define the parameters of all types of abuse, including emotional maltreatment. In prevention initiatives, parents and other caretakers can be educated on the emotional needs of children as well as the effects and damage that emotional maltreatment can cause to children both now and in the future. With quality prevention programming, a community clarifies its understanding of the problem, establishes community standards as to the appropriate emotional treatment of children, and creates a different attitude as to what is to be tolerated.

In prevention initiatives, parents and other caretakers can be educated on the … damage that emotional maltreatment can cause to children both now and in the future.

• • • • • •

The Courts and Emotional Abuse Issues

Despite the ineffectiveness of the community and child protection agencies to address emotional maltreatment as a serious threat to children, there appears to be no resistance among the courts of this country to focusing on the devastating effects of emotional maltreatment. In the following chapters, we will discuss specific emotionally abusive behaviors that damage children. We have located cases where these behaviors provided the basis for removal of children from the home or for termination of parental rights. However, before leaving this overview of the courts and abuse cases, there are categories of cases that demonstrate courts are attentive to and not at all resistant to the notion that children must be protected from emotional maltreatment. Given the fact that every adult experienced some degree of emotional abuse as a child, either at the hands of a parent or someone like a coach or teacher, it is perhaps easier for judges to empathize and relate to a child who is the victim of emotional maltreatment than physical or sexual abuse.

Let's start with language of the Supreme Court of Colorado in *People v. D.A.K., supra.* The case involved a mother in a neglect and dependency petition brought on behalf of her child. At that point, the abuse and neglect statute in Colorado stated only that a neglected or dependent child was one whose parent had subjected him to "mistreatment or abuse." The legislature had not further defined the term "abuse" and the mother contended that the term encompassed only physical abuse and not the emotional abuse with which she was primarily charged. The Court rejected this argument, stating:

> The welfare of the child cannot be protected if courts must ignore the very real emotional abuses that a child may suffer. *Emotional abuse may leave scars more permanent and damaging to a child's personality than bodily bruises from a physical beating.* Thus when the General Assembly entrusted to juvenile courts the primary responsibility for protecting neglected and dependent children, it surely intended to grant the power to protect such children against emotional abuse. [citations omitted] We decline to conclude that an enlightened legislature, which repeatedly has demonstrated its concern for children, would be concerned only with safety of the child's body, but not of the integrity of his or her mind, personality and spirit. Id. at 750. (Emphasis supplied)

The Supreme Court of Colorado makes an assertion that should be used to solidify our efforts to address the problem of emotional maltreatment. There is perhaps no stronger statement than, "Emotional abuse may leave scars more permanent and damaging to a child's personality than bodily bruises from a physical beating." It certainly is a compelling indication that the court's reaction to its responsibility in this area of child abuse should not be discounted or second-guessed.

Emotional Abuse Arising from Domestic Violence

Since the CPS system responds to child abuse, and the domestic violence system deals with spousal abuse, there is not always a sharing or coordinating of efforts to examine family violence holistically. In a typical case a mother calls law enforcement, goes to a shelter with her children where her safety is assured, and she is counseled about her future. She is the primary client in that situation. However, for several years now professionals have expressed serious concern about the children in this violent family who witness both physical and emotional battering. Prevent Child Abuse America speaks of the dangers and shares the statistic that, "Children who are abused, or who witness abuse, are six times more likely to be abusive." For this reason domestic violence cases warrant concern for the children as well as for the abused spouse.

The issue of emotional damage done to children exposed to violence has caught the attention of several courts.

The Abusive Parent in Physical Domestic Violence

The issue of emotional damage done to children exposed to violence has caught the attention of several courts. In *State ex rel. J.L.V. v. State, supra*, a father challenged the ruling of a lower court, which awarded custody of his two daughters to the children's maternal aunt and uncle. The custody battle had been triggered by the mother's suicide after years of domestic violence and threats by the father. The record demonstrated that the father had verbally and physically abused the mother in front of the children. The children had been taken into protective custody after the suicide and were found to be suffering severe emotional damage. During the custody hearing, the trial count found that the father's violent behavior toward the mother in the presence of the children "constituted emotional abuse... The emotional abuse has traumatized [the children] to the point of causing mental and emotional damage." *Id.* at 947. Based upon this finding, the trial court declined to award custody to the father. This was affirmed on appeal.

The issue of emotional damage to children resulting from viewing domestic violence has been addressed by at least one legislature.

As noted by the Supreme Court of Alaska in *A.H. v. State,* 10 P.3d 1156 (Alaska 2000):

> Alaska Statute 47.10.011(8)(B)(iii) states that a child is in need of aid when the parent has placed the child at substantial risk of mental injury as a result of "repeated exposure to conduct by a household member ... against another household member that is a crime" under domestic violence laws. *Id.* at 1161-1162.

In that case, the Supreme Court affirmed a judgment by the trial court that terminated a father's parental rights to his two children because they were neglected and had been exposed to domestic violence.

A California appellate court in *In re Heather A.,* 52 Cal.App.4th 183, 60 Cal.Rptr.2d 315 (Cal. App. 2d Dist. 1996) referred to the emotional abuse arising from witnessing domestic violence as "secondary abuse." A lower court had entered a judgment removing twin daughters from a father's custody on the basis of their exposure to the violent behavior directed at his wife. The appellate court affirmed the judgment, agreeing with the trial court that this exposure endangered the children's physical and emotional safety.

The Passive Parent in Physical Domestic Violence

Although we routinely focus on the batterer's responsibility in domestic violence cases, when children are part of the family and exposed to the atmosphere of abuse, the passive partner or victim of the physical abuse must also be seen as a parent who has responsibility to protect the child from harm.

Recently, the Supreme Court of Louisiana reviewed the effect of neglect and a parent's tolerance in allowing children to witness repeated violence in a termination case. In *State ex rel. C.J.K, supra,* the Supreme Court examined the action of the lower appellate court, which reversed a trial court finding terminating the rights of both parents because the children had suffered psychological injuries. Two children were involved in the termination petition. Their father had violently abused their mother, and the evidence showed that the children had frequently witnessed the violence.

After reviewing the trial testimony, the Supreme Court reversed the lower appellate court and reinstated the termination order entered by the trial court. In so doing, the Court said: "We conclude that the lower court erred in failing to recognize that *passive abuse or neglect by a parent can inflict just as, if not more so, "gravely disabling" injury as physical abuse.* The trial court found that [the mother's] apparent inability to protect her children from witnessing the abuse resulted in severe psychological trauma ... and properly concluded that the best interests of the children would be served in terminating both [parents'] parental rights." *Id.* at 114-115. (Emphasis supplied).

Verbal Domestic Abuse

We all would probably agree that verbal abuse generally accompanies physical domestic violence. However, serious and harmful verbal abuse may occur without any physical manifestations. The child systematically witnesses screaming, cursing, name-calling, and verbal assaults, and at times the child is encouraged to take sides and participate. The child is living in an emotionally disruptive home where the atmosphere is charged with unpredictability and uneasiness. Finally, the parents are so caught up in their own rancor that the child is left to his own devises. All of this adds up to a situation where the child's needs go unmet, and the courts have spoken to this.

...serious and harmful verbal abuse may occur without any physical manifestations.

In re: Orwell, 1993 Ohio App. LEXIS 6180 (Ohio Ct. App. Montgomery County, 1993) stands for the proposition that verbal domestic abuse can trigger a finding of emotional abuse of the children. There, the appellate court reviewed an appeal by parents of an order terminating their parental rights. A referee had been appointed to make findings of fact and a recommendation to the trial court regarding termination. The referee made the following findings:

> [T]he children were without adequate parental care due to the parents' constant fighting, bickering and arguing, in which they engaged without regard to the profound negative effect of their behavior on the children. The referee found that though the parents' outbursts were not directed at the children, the children observed these incidents and were harmed by them as the fighting was extremely disruptive and created problems for the children. The referee found that the children suffered abuse by virtual of the emotional trauma that they experienced from their parents' behavior toward each other and the parents' unwillingness to realize that the children were there and to deal with them.

After reviewing the basis for the findings, the appellate court affirmed the termination of parental rights by the trial court, finding that the parents "had exposed these children to emotional abuse from their argumentative behavior and that [the parents] were unwilling to alter their behavior in this regard...." *Id.*

The Parent's Inability to Protect a Child from Emotional Abuse

Just as with physical or sexual abuse, children who are victims of emotional maltreatment are often the object of one parent's abuse and left unprotected by the other parent who is either unwilling or unable to stop the abuse. Despite the fact that one parent does not actively abuse, the lack of protection by this parent allows the abuse to occur, and, therefore, both parents are held accountable.

This inability of one parent to protect a child from the infliction of emotional damage by another parent became a basis for finding that a child was "deprived" by the Supreme Court of North Dakota in *In Interest of N.N.*, 278 N.W.2d 150 (N.D. 1979). The case involved allegations that the mother had physically abused the daughter, but the Court was primarily concerned about the emotional health of the child at the hands of the mother. In particular, there was evidence that the child had "suffered emotional abuse by being subjected to concerted and persistent personal degradation including public embarrassment as well as being consistently called such names as 'slut' and 'whore', by her mother." *Id.* at 154. The record also confirmed that the father had done nothing to protect the child and had at times blamed the child for his own problems with the mother. The father contested the finding that his daughter was deprived as to his care, arguing that he had never physically abused the child. The Supreme Court considered his argument irrelevant to the emotional issues in the case and noted that:

Child welfare professionals have always acknowledged that, in some cases of child abuse, only one child is singled out for the abuse.

> We have held that where one parent could not prevent another parent in the home from causing a child to be deprived, the child was deprived and termination of both parent's rights were justified, notwithstanding that one parent's conduct was active and the other parent's conduct was passive. *Id.*

Accordingly, the Court affirmed the trial court's finding as to the father.

Abuse to Other Children Justifies Removal of an Unabused Child

Child welfare professionals have always acknowledged that, in some cases of child abuse, only one child is singled out for the abuse. There are many reasons for this disparity that are routinely enumerated in training and literature. However, there has been little attention given to the impact of this abuse on the other children in the home. These children may be forced to witness the abuse or even engage in the abusive behaviors, creating a serious dysfunctional situation where children are left with tremendous guilt in addition to being systematically taught to hurt.

The emotional damage done to children forced to witness abuse of a sibling was the concern of the court in *In re Edward C.*, 126 Cal.App.3d 193, 178 Cal.Rptr. 694 (Cal. App. 1st Dist. 1981). The case was triggered by reports of physical abuse from the application of excessive discipline by a father of three children. Most of the excessive discipline had been directed at the daughter. The father justified his actions as being biblically ordained and demanded by God. The daughter, who was wetting the bed, had been repeatedly beaten on her bare flesh and made to endure such punishments as having to sleep in her underwear on a plastic sheet on the floor without bedding in 60° weather. The daughter was removed from the home and adopted by her grandmother.

The remaining concern for the court was the future of the girl's brothers. Both had been physically disciplined, although not to the degree of brutality sustained by their sister. The appellate court approved removal of the boys, stating:

> [T]here is evidence that the boys not only watched the vicious treatment of their eight-year-old sister, but were admonished that the beatings were on the command of the Lord. It is difficult to conceive that the brothers could not be emotionally or psychologically scarred by witnessing the constant acts of cruelty upon their sister and upon each other; it is reasonable to infer that continued exposure to the threat of physical force will inhibit the healthy emotional development necessary to a progression from childhood to independent manhood. 126 Cal.App.3d at 204.

The courts have also accepted the concept that, if one or more children in the family have been found to be abused, that alone is evidence adequate to remove other children from the home and, indeed, to terminate parental rights to children not shown to have suffered the same abuse. This has even been applied to children born after the termination of rights to other children.

In *E.J.R. v. Young (In re J.R.), supra,* the Supreme Court of Vermont was asked to decide whether the family court had correctly ruled that a newborn child could be removed from a home where there was a long history of abusive behavior by the father and refusal by the mother to acknowledge a problem or to protect the other children. Procedurally, the question was whether a newborn could be adjudicated as a child in need of supervision (CHINS) without any evidence of actual abuse. At the time that J.R. was born, a hearing on termination of the parental rights of her four siblings had already occurred; termination as to the other children was ordered shortly after her birth. A CHINS petition was filed on the day J.R. was born, and after an emergency hearing, custody of J.R. was transferred to the Department. The parents petitioned for a writ of habeas corpus, contending that there was no evidence that J.R. had been abused or neglected and arguing that the CHINS petition had been improperly granted. The Supreme Court disagreed, stating that: "Actual and completed harmful acts cannot be, and are not, a precondition to a CHINS finding." *Id.* at 223. The Court reviewed case law from other states and cited opinions from the courts of Colorado, California, Montana, Nebraska, New York and South Dakota, all of which had reached a similar conclusion. The Court found that "there was more than sufficient evidence strongly linking the treatment of J.R.'s siblings to her own likely future treatment, justifying the order that she is a CHINS."

A similar result was reached in *Director of the Dallas County Child Protective Services Unit of the Texas Department of Human Services v. Bowling,* 833 S.W.2d 730 (Tex. App. Dallas 1992). The appellate court held a father's rights to a child born while he was in jail could be terminated. The father had violated a parole agreement and left a drug rehabilitation program, during which time he sexually abused his eighteen-month-old son. The court found that the law of Texas did not require that a child needed to be a victim of abuse before a parent's rights could be involuntarily terminated. What was necessary was adequate evidence of a course of conduct that had the effect of "jeopardizing a child's physical and emotional well-being." 833 S.W.2d at 734.

Although courts in some states led the way in determining that abuse to siblings could be adequate evidence to terminate the rights to a sibling who had not been abused by interpreting the intent of the legislature, some states have now legislated that contingency by enacting laws requiring removal.

• • • • • •

The Courts and Emotional Neglect Issues

Although neglect was the first type of child welfare case to be routinely investigated and brought to the attention of the court, it can be a very difficult concept when the neglect is emotional in nature. Neglect is by definition something that is not occurring, a passive harm. Nevertheless, the failure to provide for the emotional health of a child is as harmful as the lack of food, clothing and shelter. We know that a child must have food and a warm coat, and, regardless whether the caretaker means to hurt or not, we will demand that these basic needs be provided. The same is true for emotional needs, and courts have agreed.

> ...the failure to provide for the emotional health of a child is as harmful as the lack of food, clothing and shelter.

Emotional Neglect Not Required to Be Purposeful

In *In re C.A.R, supra*, the Supreme Court of Montana affirmed the termination of parental rights in a case that revolved around the issue of physical and emotional neglect. The Court noted the policy set out in the statute that the legislature intended to "insure that all youth are afforded an adequate physical and emotional environment to promote normal development." *Id.* at 1219. The Court acknowledged the presumption that a child should be with his parents but noted: "[W]hen the rights of a youth to an adequate physical and emotional environment encounter demonstrated acts of commission or omission by the parents which deprive the youth of this environment, the best interest of the youth is paramount and takes precedence over parental rights or familial bonds." *Id.* After reviewing all of the evidence that had been presented to the lower court, the Supreme Court found clear and convincing evidence that the children had been abused and neglected. In particular, the Court noted: "[The mother's] failure to care and attend to [her children] caused the physical problems such as excessive illness, flattened heads and uncharacteristic listlessness. *The greatest injury to the children, though, was to their cognitive and emotional development.*" *Id.* at 1220 (Emphasis supplied). The Court further noted that an examining psychiatrist had testified "[the mother's] basic problem was a lack of motivation towards her children, an inability to comprehend their needs, and a lack of depth of maturity to bring about the needed change." *Id.* at 1221. Based upon the extensive evidence of the acts of omissions of the parent, the neglect arising from them and a proven inability to understand or change behaviors, the Supreme Court terminated the parental rights.

Similarly, in *State v. Eventyr J.*, 120 N.M. 463, 902 P.2d 1066 (Ct.App. 1995), the appellate court reviewed the long history of a mother's unwillingness to provide consistent care to her four children, a history that had led a lower court to terminate her rights. The record contained a longstanding pattern of inappropriate parenting. The lower court had found that the mother had

> emotionally abused and neglected her children by the combined effect of: (1) leaving them unattended for long periods of time, (2) exposing them to dangerous situations, (3) failing to understand their physical and emotional needs, (4) failing to empathize with their feelings, (5) being self-centered in her interactions with them, (6) exposing them to domestic violence, (7) exposing them to substance abuse, (8)

> showing an indifference to their needs in favor of her own, and (9) placing them with inappropriate caretakers. *Id.* at 1071.

The appellate court affirmed the termination, noting that the mother "failed to understand her children's physical and emotional needs and consistently put her own needs ahead of those of the children… . [Mother's] inability to learn to provide the care necessary for her children's well-being is clear and convincing evidence of neglect." *Id.* at 1073.

In Texas, the termination statute allows for involuntary termination if it is found that the parent "knowingly place or knowingly allowed the child to remain in conditions or surroundings that endanger the physical and emotional well-being of the child." Tex.Fam.Code Ann §15.02(1)(d). In construing the meaning of "endanger," Texas courts have stated repeatedly that the term means to expose to loss or injury, or to jeopardize. *Texas Dep't of Human Services v. Boyd,* 727 S.W.2d, 531, 30 Tex.Sup.Ct.J. 352 (Tex. 1987). The Texas Supreme Court, in *Boyd,* also noted that the conduct need not be directed at the child or that the child actually suffer injury, but if a course of conduct is demonstrated that endangers a child's physical or emotional well-being, termination can be ordered. *Id.* at 533-534. The behavior in question might be violent or negligent, directed at the other parent or another child and even outside of the presence of the child and still be grounds for termination on an endangerment consideration. *Navarrette v. Texas Dep't. of Human Resources,* 669 S.W.2d 849 (Tex.App. El Paso 1984).

Emotional Neglect Due to Mental Illness

The ability of a parent to appropriately care for, supervise, and protect a child is always an issue to CPS, the community, and eventually the court. If there is a lack of care for the child, it is much easier to deal with it if there is demonstrated intent. We all can feel a sense of justice and satisfaction when we protect a child from a parent who is knowingly cruel or brutal toward a child.

However, we waver in our resolve when the parent has mental disabilities that he or she cannot help. In many ways, the parent appears to be a victim also. Here, intent of the parent as well as the parent's rights must be set aside to first address the child's safety and best interests, no matter how undeserving the outcome is for the parent.

...intent of the parent as well as the parent's rights must be set aside to first address the child's safety and best interests, no matter how undeserving the outcome is for the parent.

Courts have placed children first in cases involving emotional neglect in circumstances where the parent is not able to appropriately care for a child due to the parent's mental illness. In *Parker v. Department. of Pensions and Sec.*, 437 So.2d 551 (Ala. Civ. App. 1983), the appellate court approved the termination of parental rights when the evidence revealed that the mother had been diagnosed with an "anti-social personality" and where all of her children evidenced significant emotional problems.

In *A.H. v. State, supra*, the Supreme Court of Alaska affirmed the termination of parental rights to a father's two daughters because the children had been neglected; the children were at risk of mental injury because of repeated exposure to domestic violence; and the children were at substantial risk of physical and mental injury because of the father's mental illness (paranoid schizophrenia). The Supreme Court noted with regard to the issue of mental illness in a termination proceeding:

> [W]hile mental illness alone cannot form the basis of a termination order, when the record links the [parent's] continuing mental illness with his past instances of extreme neglect there may be a basis for finding that 'improper parental conduct [is] likely to continue.' [citation omitted] *Id.* at 1162.

The appellate court wrote that the lower court had found that the father's "mental illness impairs his ability to parent. Given the children's vulnerability due to their young age and developmental disabilities, his mental illness has resulted in a substantial risk of physical and mental injury to the children while they were in his care..." *Id.*

The Supreme Court of North Dakota in *Interest of D.,* 253 N.W.2d 870 (N.D. 1977) affirmed the termination of parental rights of a mother who suffered from schizophrenia. The Court found that

> the record establishes by clear and convincing evidence that [the child] was subjected to severe mental and emotional abuse from 1971 until she was removed from [her mother's] custody.... because [she] ... was being raised in an environment which encompassed her mother's attempts at suicide, talk of death, mistrust of social service help and psychiatric help, and other less serious manifestations of her mother's mental illness... . [W]e find that the State has established by clear and convincing evidence that [the mother] is now and probably will continue to be unable to provide a suitable mental and emotional environment for the growth and development of a minor child. *Id.* at 876.

The Supreme Court of South Dakota in *In re S.L.*, 419 N.W.2d 689 (S.D. 1988) detailed the evidence that led it to affirm the termination of parental rights. The parents had two children. The mother was diagnosed schizophrenic. She had a habit of locking her son into his room at night, had frequently shut him in a closet and called him dirty names. She had mutilated some of her son's personal possessions in his presence. She admitted that voices were telling her to cut her son with a knife and burn him. The mother was also found to be ignoring her infant daughter for long periods of time (up to eight hours without feeding or changing during the day). Upon evaluation, mental health professionals testified that the children had significant mental delays and psychological and emotional problems. Based upon this evidence, the lower court determined that the children's "environment was injurious to their welfare" and the children had "sustained emotional harm or mental injury." The Supreme Court affirmed that decision.

In *In re Gentry*, 142 Mich.App. 701, 369 N.W.2d 889 (Mich.App. 1985), the Court of Appeals of Michigan reviewed a challenge to that part of the termination statute that provided for termination if a parent was unable to provide proper care and custody for a child because of a "mental deficiency or mental illness" without a reasonable expectation of assuming care within a reasonable length of time. The trial court terminated the mother's parental rights due to her mental illness. The mother argued on appeal that the standard for termination due to mental illness was unconstitutionally vague. The appellate court noted that the statute did not permit termination merely because of the mental illness of a parent. "[I]t links the parent's mental illness to that parent's ability to provide proper care for the child. [citation omitted] Consequently, even if "mental illness" is subject to differing interpretations, the requirement that the condition be substantial, prolonged, and adversely affect parenting ability limits termination to cases involving severe psychological disorders." *Id.* 895-896. In this case, the court noted evidence of:

The appellate court noted that the statute did not permit termination merely because of the mental illness of a parent.

> a 20-year history of serious mental problems, which included several commitments to mental institutions, an inability to remember the names of her children, failure to understand that a college education for a four-month-old was inappropriate, and an inability to distinguish fantasy from reality. *Id.* at 894.

Accordingly, the appellate court affirmed the order terminating parental rights.

A recent development in the area of termination of rights due to emotional injuries inflicted upon a child because of the parents' mental illness is the implications of the Americans with Disabilities Act (ADA). The Supreme Court of Arkansas reviewed the arguments of a mother who contended that she had been not been provided with "reasonable accommodations" by DHS in light of her "disability," i.e. her mental illness. *J.T. v. Arkansas Dep't of Human Serv.*, 329 Ark. 243, 947 S.W.2d 761 (Ark. 1997) This was a case of first impression on this issue and the Court looked to other jurisdictions for guidance. It found that courts had generally ruled that the ADA had no impact on the court's primary focus, which was whether the child was being afforded adequate parenting. The Court noted the following from *Stone v. Daviess County Div. Child Servs.*, 656 N.E.2d 824 (Ind. Ct. App. 1995): "[I]n the final analysis, the rights of the parents under the Fourteenth Amendment and the ADA must be subordinated to the protected rights of the children." *Id.* at 831. The Supreme Court of Arkansas agreed with the Indiana court and held that, at most, the ADA impacted a termination case only in determining whether the services offered to the parents were appropriate in light of their disability. The Court found:

A recent development in the area of termination of rights due to emotional injuries inflicted upon a child because of the parents' mental illness is the implications of the Americans with Disabilities Act (ADA).

> We thus conclude that [mother] has failed to demonstrate that her rights pursuant to the ADA were violated by either DHS, Dr. Brown, or the trial court. [M]other was not denied any services on the basis of

> her mental disability; rather, the trial court's denial of visitation with [daughter] was motivated solely by what the court deemed was in the best interest of the emotionally fragile child. 947 S.W.2d at 768.

Emotional Neglect Due to Addictions

Over the last forty years the issue of parental addiction to alcohol and/or drugs has emerged as a major problem for the community and all agencies seeking to serve children. In the first place, the stereotypical drunk before 1960 was a male. Today, alcoholism is no longer a gender specific problem. This change, added to the tremendous increase in one-parent homes, has created a new, emerging problem of addiction to alcohol by the only parent.

The use of heroin, crack cocaine, illegal prescription drugs, paint thinner, and other mood or mind altering substances has certainly exacerbated the problem of child abuse and family violence. The procurement and use of drugs creates an atmosphere in the home where children are involved in criminal activity and the atmosphere that goes with it. In addition, a parent whose attention is focused on maintaining a drug habit is not giving the attention, care and supervision required by a child. Neglect is a very valid concern in such households.

The use of heroin, crack cocaine, illegal prescription drugs, paint thinner, and other mood or mind altering substances has certainly exacerbated the problem of child abuse and family violence.

As the drug problem escalated over the last forty years to an epidemic level, the CPS system was certainly overwhelmed with the fallout. They had to deal with child abandonment, incarcerated parents and drug-addicted babies. Looking at the emotional effects of parental addiction to alcohol and/or drugs was not a priority. The proliferation of child abuse in general, coupled with the same or shrinking financial resources, pushed the CPS system to create priorities and go to a risk assessment approach to investigation. This response was certainly provoked by the overwhelming number of cases reported after the 1975 federal mandates even without the exacerbation caused by drugs. The resulting triage approach left little room to deal with anything but the most heinous parental behaviors. Emotional neglect, as a result of alcohol or drug addiction, was just too rampant to address in many communities.

> Courts have been concerned where one or both parents are so caught up in their addictions that they neglect the care of their children.

Despite this, when the issue of parental addition does come to the attention of the court, there has been a willingness on the part of judges to act on behalf on the child. Courts have been concerned where one or both parents are so caught up in their addictions that they neglect the care of their children. Recently, in *Doe v. Doe (In re Doe),* 133 Idaho 805, 992 P.2d 1205 (Idaho 1999), the Supreme Court of Idaho terminated the rights of a mother who had repeatedly violated the terms of a series of orders defining her obligations if she wanted to continue to have visitation rights with her daughter. Through several modifications of the orders, the mother was found to have continued to consume alcohol and illegal drugs in front of the child and to have consistently been unable to change her addictive behaviors. When her child was staying with her, the mother had been found intoxicated and passed out with the child crying and trying to wake her up. She did not take care of the child, and others had to feed and dress her daughter when she was under the influence of alcohol and drugs. The trial court's decision that it would be the best interests of the child to terminate the mother's parental relationship was affirmed.

In another recent Idaho case, the Idaho Court of Appeals in *Department of Health & Welfare v. Doe (In re Doe),* 133 Idaho 826,

992 P.2d 1226 (Idaho Ct. Appeals 1999) affirmed the termination of parental rights of a mother addicted to drugs. Her child had been born with traces of methamphetamine and had been taken into custody at birth. In Idaho, the presence of the drug in the baby resulted in this mother being charged with criminal injury to a child, a charge to which she pleaded guilty. After the mother was placed on probation, she failed to complete a chemical dependency program and violated probation frequently. The department moved to terminate the mother's parental rights on a neglect petition. The mother argued that she could not be charged with neglect because the child had been in the custody of the department since birth. The appellate court found that neglect is a permissible ground for termination for a noncustodial parent and that the mother's failure to fulfill or remotely comply with a reunification plan or attempt to assume parental responsibilities supported a finding of neglect. The appellate court also agreed with the trial court's finding that it was in the best interests of the child that termination occur.

...CPS and the courts must become more proactive in intervening quickly in order to give the children of addicts a chance for normal physical, mental and emotional growth.

There is no doubt that, with the explosion of serious addictions to cocaine and other drugs, and with a better understanding of the effects of neglect on the brain development of young children, CPS and the courts must become more proactive in intervening quickly in order to give the children of addicts a chance for normal physical, mental and emotional growth.

Since resulting behaviors may not be recognized as connected to emotionally abusive actions, we often get the consequences of emotional abuse without being able to relate them to parental behaviors and statements.

Chapter Nine

Operational Categories of Emotional Maltreatment

In 1985, a group of professionals from across the nation were asked to participate in a federal-state project funded by the National Center on Child Abuse and Neglect and the states of Alabama, Mississippi, Vermont, Maine, and Virginia. The purpose of this early, important project was to develop operational definitions of emotional maltreatment. Project directors were the late Thelma F. Baily, MSS, and Walter H. Baily, Ph.D., of Limerick, Maine.

One of the authors was a participant in this project, and the following chapters are a broad discussion of the findings and implications of the research. Despite the fact that this research was done some years ago, the value of it remains constant. There is little other definitive material on the subject, especially in this much detail. In addition, as professionals in child welfare and other related fields have begun to look at risk factors in families that may indicate a high propensity for abuse, especially the absence of empathy, the material in the NCCAN study has taken on new and significant meaning.

The *Final Report* of this project, published in May 1986, includes the following introductory statement:

> The abuse behaviors by caretakers may cause no observable physical changes, except in the very young child, but the resultant personality damage is often difficult to deny. A non-assertive, apprehensive, self-doubting, insecure youth who attempts to commit suicide, who has no friends and seems to want none, who

> cannot perform in school, but has average intelligence, will not be described as a healthy person who can cope with many facets of adult life. When it is known that the youth has been exposed to parents who have ignored him, who have rejected all his attempts to learn, accomplish and perform, and who have belittled and ridiculed him, it is difficult to escape the conclusion of the relationship between the two sets of behaviors. (Baily & Baily, 1986)

This project set out to develop a consensus on a set of parental behaviors that would likely result in emotional impairment of a child. The discussions among participants in this study produced a list of parental behaviors that could impair healthy child emotional development. These behaviors were grouped into clusters according to the age of the child, taking into consideration the unique characteristics of children in the preschool, latency, and adolescent periods. Despite some differences, a set of parental behaviors emerged that basically cut across all ages.

Arguably, two methods for identifying emotional maltreatment exist.

Just as child welfare practice examined parental behaviors that were harmful to the child, the research group was able to come to agreement on parental behaviors that would be emotionally abusive or neglectful. Since resulting behaviors may not be recognized as connected to emotionally abusive actions, we often get the consequences of emotional abuse without being able to relate them to parental behaviors and statements. Arguably, two methods for identifying emotional maltreatment exist. One, we can observe and test children to determine if they demonstrate deficits in their normal emotional development and then look at the relationship between the parent and child to identify the basis for the deficits. Two, we can observe parental behaviors that we have come to recognize as destructive to a child's normal development, and then take a close look at how those behaviors are impacting the child. In either scenario, the authors of the study recognized that we must identify, discuss, and become comfortable with the whole panoply of parental actions that cause emotional maltreatment.

The project directors took input from all participants and grouped the behaviors under an overall definitional statement. Some of these behaviors constitute a failure to provide necessary care that children need, while others are behaviors that are overt in nature. Although there are no absolute guidelines for the clustering of these behaviors, the individual behaviors identified by the participants appear to group themselves around five categories of emotional maltreatment identified by an early researcher in this field. Once again, we turn to Dr. James Garbarino, who has traditionally grouped his discussion of emotional abuse around the areas of ignoring, isolating, rejecting, terrorizing, and corrupting. (Garbarino & Garbarino, 1994) Professionals appear to be comfortable with using these categories in discussing emotionally abusive and neglectful behaviors that pull against an environment children need in order to be emotionally healthy.

This child is what was once called a "cipher" or zero, one who for all practical purposes does not exist as far as the parent or caretaker is concerned.

Ignoring

This category of emotional maltreatment is generally passive in nature and falls into the neglect area. In other words, the adult fails to give the attention needed by the child. This child is what was once called a "cipher" or zero, one who for all practical purposes does not exist as far as the parent or caretaker is concerned. There is little or no emotional connection, appropriate communication, or response given to the child. This is one area of emotional maltreatment where intent may not be present.

Isolating

This category of maltreatment focuses on cutting the child off from others. The isolation may be physical, emotional, or both. Regardless of whether it is physical or emotional, this maltreatment is usually an overt act on the part of the adult, allegedly to serve as punishment. It may be a physical act such as placing the child in a closet, or it may be an emotional act such as prohibiting the family to look at or interact with the child. Isolation also may involve prohibiting the child from having contact with anyone outside the home.

Rejecting

This category of maltreatment may be abusive or neglectful depending on the situation. For example, if the parent refuses any attempt of the child to be close or withholds affection, then it is basically neglectful or passive. However, if the rejection takes the form of overt statements that are cruelly critical of the child and his or her value, then abuse may be the better term. Either way it is a "pushing away" of the child and denial of necessary acceptance.

Terrorizing

This type of emotional abuse could be called psychological battering or assault. It is generally seen as the set of behaviors used in prisoner-of-war compounds where fear for bodily harm or other pain is used to effect compliance or acquiescence. Although there may be no actual physical mutilation, the POW knows that the threat can become reality because his captors have total power over him. In this category of emotional maltreatment, threats of heinous physical harm or outcomes for the child are used by the adult to maintain control and/or punish the child.

...threats of heinous physical harm or outcomes for the child are used by the adult to maintain control and/or punish the child.

Corrupting

Society places upon parents the responsibility to teach a child what is right and wrong, both in a legal and a moral or ethical sense. The corruption category involves such a failure of this parental task that a child suffers emotional damage because he will not be capable of interacting appropriately with the world. Passively neglecting to teach legal and ethical boundaries through basic irresponsibility would be emotional neglect. If the parent overtly teaches or requires a child to perform unlawful or immoral acts, or routinely models these acts for the child, those behaviors would be seen as emotional abuse.

Passively neglecting to teach legal and ethical boundaries through basic irresponsibility would be emotional neglect.

• • • • • •

These five areas of emotional maltreatment are broad and may be applied to cover most unacceptable behaviors that adults demonstrate toward children that fall outside the confines of physical and sexual abuse and physical neglect. One or more of these behaviors may be found in the same family, for they frequently overlap and thrive together. They can also exist where no physical or sexual abuse occurs. Although the behaviors are often found in situations where physical and/or sexual abuse is present, we will be looking at them as they stand alone in causing emotional abuse or neglect. The legal cases used to illustrate the intervention of CPS and the courts because of these parental behaviors involve situations where the sole or primary concern is emotional harm done to children.

In the final report from the study, the behaviors were grouped by pre-school, latency, or adolescence. A majority of the behaviors cut across all three categories. All of the behaviors associated with the latency period will be presented in the next chapters, followed by a discussion of a behavior peculiar to preschool.

Studies of ignored children in institutions describe emotional neglect so severe that infant mortality was more than 33 percent.

Chapter Ten

Operational Definitions: Ignoring

> **DEFINITION**
>
> ***The parent shows no attachment to the child and fails to provide nurturance.***

Possible Parental Behaviors

The parent typically fails to call the child to meals, wake him/her up in the morning, recognize his/her presence, keep promises or agreements, or otherwise act as if he/she is a member of the family. The parent almost never listens to the child's questions, fails to give praise for accomplishments and almost never asks about or shows an interest in the child's welfare. Conversation with the child is confined to giving orders, demanding or criticizing.

Implications

This child can be ignored to the point that he almost doesn't exist within the family. In the past professionals have referred to children in extreme cases of ignoring as ciphers or zeros. He or she is just not there.

In infants and young children who are physically dependent on the parent for nourishment, clothing, hygiene, supervision, and stimulation, the parent who ignores the child and neglects to provide adequate care endangers the life of the child. Studies of ignored children in institutions describe emotional neglect so severe that infant mortality was more than 33 percent. Although the death rate among children in their own home due to emotional deprivation is not as high, the number of failure-to-thrive cases is growing. (Monteleone, 1996)

Although the death rate among children in their own home due to emotional deprivation is not as high, the number of failure-to-thrive cases is growing.

As an example, parents must nurture a complex set of skills related to eating that children learn over time. Parents may give "too little support" and fail to respond to children's requests or demands for feeding, resulting in problems leading to undernutrition. "The emotional static in the interaction between parent and child may become so salient that it drowns out the child's ability to distinguish and respond to feeding cues." (Kessler & Dawson, 1999)

In other words, the parent's lack of appropriate emotional response can significantly impact the child's ability to eat and subsequently develop and thrive. Having bottles in the refrigerator is, therefore, no indication of the feeding relationship of parent and child that is so vital to the child's health. The nurturance of feeding and the related behaviors such as appropriate response, holding, patience, and encouragement all affect the growth and development of the child. Failure to attend to these needs, whether overt or neglectful, has a physical impact that may not be evident for some time in weight loss, failure to gain weight or mental development.

The routine and rhythm of life within a family involves rituals and expectations.

The routine and rhythm of life within a family involves rituals and expectations. For a child, being called to meals, asked questions, awakened in the morning, engaged in conversation, and other interactions of daily living, might not all occur every day. Generally speaking, however, within a family there are expectations of recognition and affirmation that make up the fabric of the day. This type of ignoring is a passive act of negligence, for the attention and interaction between a child and an adult are needed for normal development of social skills and confirmation of self-worth. "Studies of psychologically unavailable parents find that the children fail to thrive and develop normally. These children are both emotionally and cognitively delayed." (Monteleone, 1996)

"Studies of psychologically unavailable parents find that the children fail to thrive and develop normally. . . ."

Despite this acknowledged need for nurturance, a Michigan appellate court allowed a mother to keep her children, although there was a complete lack of bonding to them. In *In re Bedwell,* 160 Mich.App. 168, 408 N.W.2d 65 (1987), the trial court had terminated the mother's rights to her three children because she had emotionally neglected her children. The mother did not contest the allegations of emotional neglect, and the court accepted the report of a mental health professional who had determined that the children had not bonded with their mother. The expert attributed the parent's inability to bond to emotional abuse that the mother had suffered as a child.

Unfortunately, the appellate court reversed the termination of rights, taking the position that the "lack of a positive parental bond between a respondent and a minor child does not constitute emotional neglect under the statute when it is not the result of a culpable act or omission on the part of the parent.... [T]he failure to bond did not result from respondent-mother's disregard of her duty to provide emotional care, but resulted from her inability to provide emotional care. The evidence does not reveal a culpable or blameworthy act or omission by respondent-mother." *Id.* at 68. A dissent (J.M. Batzer, J) filed in the case saw the standard to be applied quite differently:

> The record here shows respondent-mother is "emotionally disturbed" and incapable of providing emotional warmth and love to these children. Her condition may well not be her "fault" to a treating psychologist in that her condition had its origins in childhood circumstances she could not control. But is not the same true for a character-disordered abuser of children? Is such a person then without fault or culpability in juvenile court proceedings? Cannot the juvenile court act in the face of serious threats to the future welfare of the child where there is a real evidence of long-term neglect—as measured by the needs of the child? I would so measure neglect—more by the needs of the child and less by the fault, culpability or blameworthiness of the parent. *Id.* at 70.

In this case the majority determined that the critical inquiry was whether the mother intended to cause harm. Her inability to appropriately parent was allowed to override the needs of her children.

The outcome of this 1987 case should be different today in light of the CAPTA requirements that the effect of behavior on, and the risk to, the child is what is critical. The new research on the effect of emotional neglect on the needs of children would also lead to a different result.

DEFINITION

The parent expresses no affection toward the child and avoids and resists all physical closeness such as hugging, touching, or smiling.

Possible Parental Behaviors

Whenever the child asks the parent for assistance, he/she is either ignored, told to keep quiet, told to come back later or told to leave the area. The parent typically speaks to the child only to give orders, criticize, accuse or demand.

Implications

The intimacy of interaction between parent and child is lacking or non-existent. The only situation that evokes a response is when the parent feels that the child has committed an error, messed up, or did not please the parent or someone the parent wishes to please or impress.

This behavior cluster also frequently has an element of rejection since closeness and physical touching are normally identified by many people with confirmation and acceptance. Realizing that in some family systems there is an established, if not spoken, code that states, "We are not an affectionate or demonstrative family. It doesn't mean we don't love each other," one must consider if the child agrees with this family behavior. Is this a parental edict or value that precludes the wishes or needs of the child? This is especially important if the child sees other children embraced and receiving affection either in his/her friend's homes or on TV.

Of course, the more serious situation involves the withholding of affection to one child of a sibling group. This personal ignoring of one child would cause hurt, feelings of alienation and anger. We have seen parental behavior in some cases of physical neglect where one child receives more food, clothes or special belongings than another child in the home. It follows, therefore, that emotional neglectful behavior could occur in a similar manner where one child receives attention and confirmation, and another child is ignored or rejected. This creates an

...emotional neglectful behavior could occur in a similar manner where one child receives attention and confirmation, and another child is ignored or rejected.

emotionally difficult situation for both children. The one who is neglected suffers a lack of the emotional nurturing needed for healthy growth and development. The one who is favored may have feelings of misplaced guilt. The preferred sibling, on the other hand, may feel lucky or superior. However, this child is a part of the abusive behavior and is developing unacceptable feelings of entitlement that will be cause problems in the future.

The other behavior in this group that implicates rejection as well as ignoring or lack of affection concerns a more active element of emotional abuse.

The other behavior in this group that implicates rejection as well as ignoring or lack of affection concerns a more active element of emotional abuse. Here the parent withholds the positive such as hugging, but pours on the negative that includes regular and extreme criticism, constant demands and unfounded accusations.

This type of behavior that both ignores and rejects a child's need for positive attention was exhibited by a mother in *Cynthia C. v. Superior Court,* 72 Cal.App.4th 1196, 85 Cal.Rptr.2d 669 (Cal.App. 4th Dist. 1999). Procedurally, the case involved the attempt by a parent to reverse her previous consent to waiving her parental rights to her daughter. The child was her oldest; she also had two children by a second marriage. The family and the child had been receiving services but:

> in spite of this assistance, the parents were openly hostile toward Christina. Both the parents' therapist and Christina's therapist concluded they were emotionally abusive to her. The parents attributed her problem behaviors, including lying and stealing, impulsivity, hyperactivity, somatic complaints, explosive tantrums, fearfulness, and inability to respond

> to directions and separation difficulties to "planned deviousness" on seven-year-old Christina's part.
>
> In response to these behaviors, Christina was assessed for attention deficit hyperactivity disorder (ADHD) by two psychiatrists. Both concluded her behavior was more likely attributable to anxiety stemming from emotional abuse and neglect rather than ADHD...
>
> On August 10, 1998, Christina struck both Cynthia [her mother] and her half brother. Cynthia then called Phillipson [case worker] and asked her to remove Christina from the home. When Phillipson arrived, Cynthia stated in Christina's presence that she was afraid of her daughter, she loved her but had to think about the rest of the family; and she was at the 'end of her rope." Cynthia informed Phillipson she had consulted with Henry [step father] and they agreed Christina should be removed and placed for adoption...
>
> Phillipson urged Cynthia to reconsider for a few days, but she insisted Christina should be removed immediately. During this exchange Christina clung to her mother, crying and pleading, "Give me another chance. I will be good. Please don't give me up." Phillipson had to spend several hours with Christina until she was calm enough to be brought into protective custody. *Id.* at 1198.

After Christina was removed from the home, CPS filed a petition alleging that the child had been abandoned and emotionally abused. Cynthia offered to immediately sign a relinquishment for adoption and her waiver of rights to reunification services was repeated in court. Papers confirming the waiver were signed a month after the removal. Five months later, Cynthia requested a withdrawal of her waiver. This had occurred after her family had ostracized Cynthia at Christmas for giving Christina up for adoption. The Court requested CPS to evaluate the effect of allowing Cynthia to change her mind. The following was reported to the Court: "Phillipson noted Christina was doing very well in her prospective adoptive home. Although she still had behavior problems, they had lessened to a great degree. Christina referred to her caretakers as "mom and pop," and they were already engaged in therapy with her. Phillipson believed Christina would be emotionally devastated if her parents were reintroduced into her life after rejecting her." *Id.* at 1199. Based on this evidence, the lower court refused to allow Cynthia to withdraw her waiver.

"...Christina would be emotionally devastated if her parents were reintroduced into her life after rejecting her."

On appeal, Cynthia contended that the lower court abused its discretion in making this ruling. The appellate court noted: "If the context were not so sad, the notion would be laughable." *Id.* at 1120. Looking at the record of emotional abuse and the fact that Cynthia had knowingly and voluntarily signed the waiver even after she had supposedly had a change of mind, the court stated that "it would have been an abuse of discretion to order reunification services" and denied Cynthia's petition to rescind her waiver.

This case is a graphic example of a parent's total lack of concern or value for her child except when faced with criticism or shaming from others. It is a reminder that intent plays more than one role in the evaluation of child abuse. We

This case is a graphic example of a parent's total lack of concern or value for her child except when faced with criticism or shaming from others.

struggle with whether or not a parent intends to harm a child, but perhaps we should also examine intent in another context. Why does a parent really want to keep a child when many indications show that she or he is not bonded to the child, and there is little respect or value placed on the child by the parent? Assuming that parental ties, natural instincts, parental inclinations, or the "natural order of things" supercede the selfish or narcissistic motives of a parent could be a serious mistake and place the child in a situation that is severely damaging.

Why does a parent really want to keep a child when many indications show that she or he is not bonded to the child, and there is little respect or value placed on the child by the parent?

..."troubled parents sometimes vent their woes to their children, especially children who seem mature for their years. But serious adult problems are almost always too much for a young soul to manage."

Chapter Eleven

Operational Definitions: Isolating

DEFINITION

The parent makes inappropriate demands on and exploits the child by expecting the child to take care of the parent, to be a companion, to protect the parent from outsiders, and to perform household tasks/functions that the parent is unwilling to do.

Possible Parental Behaviors

The child is used as a spy, ally or confidante in the parent's romantic relationships, marital or divorce problems and, as a result, is frequently caught in verbal battles between and among adults. Excessive household and adult responsibilities are consistently demanded of the child. As a result of all these parental functions that the child must perform, he/she is often kept home from school and is unable to take part in peer activities for social development.

Implications

This cluster of parental behaviors captures situations where family roles are blurred, casting children in inappropriate and potentially harmful adult roles. Circumstances such as single parenthood, isolation, lack of other supportive relationships, or merely lethargy may cause the parent to turn to the child as a "best friend" or pal. Regardless of the reason and generally over time, in these situations the child/parent relationship changes to benefit the parent's needs for friendship, intimacy and support.

These behaviors have many negative outcomes for the child. In the first place, if the child is involved in adult concerns, activities, and responsibilities, he/she is not working through the normal childhood processes that are appropriate for his/her age. For example, the twelve-year-old boy who is busy accompanying the parent to adult hangouts, visiting acquaintances or cruising to check on the parent's boyfriends is not outside with the guys playing touch football, playing hide-and-seek, or talking with girls.

In combative divorce or separations the child is an easy pawn to be used by the caretaker parent in particular. The child is visiting in the non-custodial parent's home and is solicited as a spy to report back. "Is she sleeping in the same bed with your father?" is often a question. "What all has he bought her?" could be another. A conspiratorial alliance forms between the parent and child to benefit the parent's desire for information, revenge, or control.

In the period immediately following a separation and before a divorce sets out final custody arrangements, child support, etc., the child may be at extreme risk as he/she is pulled back and forth between the two fighting parents who both seek to use him/her as a pawn, collateral, or wedge in the on-going conflict. The child may never be struck or physically abused, but the threats, game playing and schemes often force the child to take sides or even participate in these subterfuges.

The child may never be struck or physically abused, but the threats, game playing and schemes often force the child to take sides or even participate in these subterfuges.

Secondly, there must be an examination of the sexual implications of the parent/child role, especially where it is mother/son or father/daughter. The boy can easily see himself as the "man of the house" or the girl as the "woman of the house." Whether or not there is any actual sexual contact or involvement, the child can certainly be misled as to his/her role with the parent. Especially with children in latency, where this relationship is normally confusing, this could be particularly harmful.

After receiving a child abuse report from a divorced father, CPS investigated allegations involving Kevin, a ten-year-old boy. The mother admitted that she and Kevin slept together, but denied, as did he, that there had been any sexual contact. However, in the numerous interviews, Kevin made statements such as, "My mother needs me. She can't make it without me. I have to take care of her." His schoolwork had suffered; he had no friends and found it difficult to talk about "boy" topics.

If a young boy "takes over" the father's role in the home, and the mother later meets and forms a relationship with an adult male, the propensity for problems in the home is great.

If a young boy "takes over" the father's role in the home, and the mother later meets and forms a relationship with an adult male, the propensity for problems in the home is great. The result can be anger, acting out toward the new male "father figure" and other destructive behaviors such as running away.

The danger of drawing a child into the world of adult problems was the subject of an editorial published in *The Spokesman-Review* (Spokane, Washington, October 4, 1997). The editorial discussed the damage a troubled adult could do to a child. At a trial of a junior high student who had shot and killed three classmates, the child's mother stated that she "confided her problems to her son from the time he was quite small. She admitted she sometimes kept him home from kindergarten for his companionship. She did not shield him from her dark moods and he would often find her in bed, deep in depression. 'He was my best friend,' she told the court." The editorial made the point that "troubled parents sometimes vent their woes to their children, especially children who seem mature for their years. But serious adult problems are almost always too much for a young soul to manage."

There may be corrupting aspects to this cluster of behaviors also. When the child is cast in the role of protector of the parent, he/she may be expected to lie or perform duties that are unacceptable for a child. Here the parent says, "Answer the phone and tell my boss that I am sick." Another possibility is, "Here's ten bucks, tell Billy to send me some weed." In attempts to look after the parent, the child is called upon to break the law, be deceitful or engage in other unlawful acts.

In attempts to look after the parent, the child is called upon to break the law, be deceitful or engage in other unlawful acts.

Caught up in responsibilities and thrust into the role of an adult, this child is often absent from school. He/she unnecessarily accompanies the parent to court hearings, sits around in the courthouse hall, goes to work with the parent or just stays home to keep her company and do the housework or cooking.

Several cases reflect these types of inappropriate parenting behaviors. In *In re: Kathleen R.,* 1993 Conn.Super. LEXIS 2537 (Conn.Sup.Ct., June 14, 1993) (an unreported decision)[3], the court terminated the parental rights of a mother with a history of mental problems. The trial included much expert testimony from mental health professionals who had worked with both the mother and child. One

[3]Some of the cases we use to illustrate inappropriate parental behaviors in emotional abuse and neglect scenarios are "unreported" decisions. If a case is unreported, it is not included in state or federal case law reporters that publish decisions that can be used for precedential value. States take differing approaches to unreported decisions. Some will not report a case when it merely restates settled law in the jurisdiction. Some states permit the use of an unreported decision if the text of the opinion is provided to opposing counsel and to the judge. Whether a case is unreported will be indicated in the citation–whether it can be used in a particular jurisdiction will depend on the rules enacted to cover such decisions.

therapist who had provided family therapy noted difficulties "in the mother's ability to understand Kathleen's needs and respond to them. The mother continued to discuss her sex life in the presence of the child, and told the child she was 'going to make love tonight' while singing and gyrating around the room. She found that the mother consistently acted inappropriately, swore, used obscenities and focused entirely on meeting her own needs, not the child's, while the child exhibited a great deal of anxiety and tension in the joint sessions, deteriorated and became upset." *Id.* at 11. Another therapist who oversaw interaction between mother and child testified that:

> [The mother] got angry, swore at nurses, discussed adult issues in front of the child, and did nothing to help alleviate the child's fears and anxiety. While the witness noted improvement in the child's ability to handle rules and limits, except on days her mother visited, the mother continued to be angry and confused, and displayed her anger inappropriately, which embarrassed and humiliated the child. She described the mother as being unable to provide consistent limits for the child, even in a controlled environment. *Id.* at 12-13.

In this case, the mother's inability to function as an adult places the daughter in a situation where she cannot be a child. The mother exhibits behaviors associated with an out-of-control child that not only teaches the child inappropriate behaviors but prevents the parent from giving an empathetic response to the child.

In *J.T. v. Arkansas Department of Human Services., supra,* an eleven-year-old girl had been removed from a mother who was mentally ill. At the time of the removal, the child was demonstrating symptoms that mimicked the psychotic behaviors of her mother. A therapist noted that "when [the child] is around [her mother], she exhibits characteristics of a *parentified child,* one who assumes the role of acting parent, showing more parenting skills than the mother and sometimes assuming charge of the household.... [The therapist] stated that [the child] needed closure to this situation and that the child was even at the point of trying to recruit potential parents to adopt her." 947 S.W.2d at 764. (Emphasis supplied) The trial court found

> that the mother's mental illness was a factor that caused the child to enter foster care. The Court further finds that the mother has had consistant [sic] treatment for her mental illness and will need continued treatment for the rest of her life. The child has had some psychiatric difficulties also and has improved since entering foster care. However, the Court cannot close its eyes to the fact that it must do what is in the best interest of [the child] who is entering adolescence, is parentified, and needs a parent or care giver who can be confrontive and set limits, be resistant to challenges, threats, and verbal abuse that this child can exhibit. The child also needs to definitely know what is going to happen in her life. *Id.* at 766.

Based on this review of the evidence, the trial court terminated the mother's rights, a result that was affirmed by the Supreme Court of Arkansas.

This case moves past intent, and focuses on the welfare and safety of the child. A mentally-ill parent may or may not be able to understand a child's needs and may not intend to harm the child. However, given the behaviors and limitations of the parent, the outcome is the same.

DEFINITION

The parent has consistently refused to permit any professional to assess the child's problems, and has also announced that the child is forbidden from participating in any remedial education or counseling services.

Possible Parental Behaviors

Although the child exhibits problems at school, at home and other situations necessary for his well being, and professionals such as teachers, school social workers, school psychologists, and others have asked the parent to get help for the child, the parent refuses. The parent may blame the child's problems on other factors, unable to see that regardless of the reason, the child is suffering from ostracism, failure, isolation, or other developmentally retarding conditions.

Implications

The education system is obviously most involved in this area of concern since it is here that the child first encounters the need to adjust and perform in keeping with community norms. The school sees problems and, with their federal mandate to provide appropriate educational opportunities for all children, seeks to find answers. Teachers may ask that the child be tested and/or placed in special education classes. Guidance counselors may feel the child needs counseling beyond what the school can provide, or they have reason to think that the child should be in a residential treatment program. Despite the concern and guidance of the school system, in some cases the parent refuses, leaving the child languishing in a frustrating or damaging situation.

Despite the concern and guidance of the school system, in some cases the parent refuses, leaving the child languishing in a frustrating or damaging situation.

These behaviors have similarities to cases where the parent refuses to obtain needed medical assistance for the child. These medical neglect cases have found their way into court with a variety of outcomes. There is really little difference between medical neglect and the failure of parents to provide needed emotional or mental support and treatment for children, especially since it generally can be provided without charge to the parents. The school must provide services or accommodations for the child to ensure that he has an equal opportunity to participate in the education process.

When the parent resists remedial help or support, there certainly may be a number of reasons. These may range from embarrassment, guilt, denial, or a genuine lack of confidence in the recommendation. A recommendation made under federal special education guidelines is not done without thought, evaluation and planning. Several people are routinely involved in making a plan. By the time it occurs, there have probably been numerous attempts to resolve the problems, and the child is believed to be unable to reach his potential without help. There also would be concern for the welfare of other students in the class. Regardless, this is a situation that should be reconciled, and it is the responsibility of the parent and the school to see that it is.

Caught in the bind between federal mandates and the resistance of the parent, the school must seek outside help. If the child exhibits difficulty with his psychological functioning and is not capable of performing normally, this would become the basis for a report to CPS to evaluate what is happening within the family. If the parents continue to be resistant, CPS can use the authority of the courts to order services that would include a professional assessment of what is happening in the child's life to cause the emotional deficits that isolate him from normal interactions with others.

DEFINITION

The parent denies the child the opportunity to learn from others by prohibiting the child from participating in social activities commonly engaged in by the child's peers, such as extra-curricular or outside play.

Possible Parental Behaviors

The child is consistently prohibited from playing with all or nearly all children of a similar age. The parent forces the child to "give in" in all conflicts, telling the child that he or she is always at fault.

Although the child may be innocent, the parent consistently blames him or her for any interpersonal problems he or she has with others.

Implications

This set of parental behaviors is an impediment to the normal socialization of children. By isolating the child from his peers, the parent does not allow the child to learn how to interact appropriately with others. It is in the context of play and social activities that children share, "balance their needs with the needs of others," settle disputes and handle conflict. Without this interaction, albeit troublesome and contentious, the child is unable to learn the social skills that he will need.

There are basically two reasons why parents may choose to isolate the child from peers. In some situations, the parent disapproves of other children and justifies the behavior as seeking to "protect" the child from outside influence. In cases such as this, the parent always finds fault with neighborhood children, friends at school, activities that are elective, and places roadblocks to prevent the child's participation.

The isolation that we identify as being emotionally abusive or neglectful is also identified as a characteristic of sexually abusive families. The family may have secrets that they do not wish the child to share with others, and the parent seeks to limit those opportunities. Sexual abuse is not the only reason for this behavior. The parent's use of drugs or alcohol or other socially unacceptable behaviors may also be an impetus for isolation.

The isolation that we identify as being emotionally abusive or neglectful is also identified as a characteristic of sexually abusive families.

A case that demonstrated a family's pattern of isolation and inappropriate behaviors is *Stuart v. Tarrant County Child Welfare Unit,* 677 S.W.2d 273 (Tex.. App. Fort Worth 1984). There, parents appealed from a lower court's ruling terminating their rights to their son. The parents had two other children. One of those children had died at ten months from "infant death syndrome." A daughter had died at age three from severe burns sustained in a fire in the Stuart's camper. The father was a mechanic who moved his family frequently. At the time of the fire that killed the daughter, the family was living in a camper truck, driving from town to town to sell tools at flea markets. Their daughter had been unattended in the camper when her clothing caught fire from a lighted gas stove. Paramedics took the child to a hospital where she died. The parents never went to the hospital. Instead, they packed the camper and left town. At the time of her death, the daughter weighed only seven and a half pounds. When tracked down, CPS removed their son, Jeremy, from the Stuart's custody and eventually moved to terminate their parental rights.

Although there was no evidence that Jeremy had been abused, evidence demonstrated that Jeremy was a "particularly fearful child."

The parents testified at the trial on the termination that they left town instead of seeing to their daughter because they had not enrolled Jeremy at school and feared his being taken from them. Although there was no evidence that Jeremy had been abused, evidence demonstrated that Jeremy was a "particularly fearful child." He also felt that he was in some way responsible for his sister's death. Psychological testing confirmed educational experience deprivation and language development delay caused by experience deprivation. An expert testified that Jeremy "needed to be in a stable environment in which he could attend school and develop normal relationships with other children." 677 S.W.2d at 281. Finding that the parents had "engaged in conduct dangerous to Jeremy's physical and emotional well being," the appellate court affirmed the termination judgment.

In other cases, the parent isolates the child as a punishment or a means to control or exert power over the child. "You don't deserve to play with anyone. You don't know how to behave," the parent tells the child, using social contact as leverage. Of course, when the parent tells the child that his or her behavior is unacceptable, it may or may not be true. This is because the parent's respect and value for the child is so low that he or she never takes or listens to the child's position in a conflict. Instead, the parent assumes his or her child is always at fault and places blame there.

"You don't deserve to play with anyone. You don't know how to behave," the parent tells the child, using social contact as leverage.

An interesting case out of California demonstrates a neglectful environment that separated children from the world and led to emotional injury. *In re Shelley J.*, 68 Cal.App.4th 322, 79 Cal.Rptr.2d 922 (Cal.App.6th Dist. 1998) involved a situation where the Department of Family and Children's Services became involved with a family whose fourteen-year-old daughter was a runaway. Upon investigation, the Department found the house to be piled from floor to ceiling with trash and raw garbage, with only two narrow passages from the front door to the kitchen. A second daughter, Laura, was removed from the house and found to be "dependent." With regard to Shelley, the Department filed and obtained an order finding the child to be dependent and ordering services. The basis for the petition was that the child was "suffering, or is at substantial risk of suffering, serious emotional damage evidenced by severe anxiety, depression, withdrawal, or untoward aggressive behavior toward self or others." The mother appealed the order.

The appellate court looked at the record of the circumstances found by the Department and affirmed the order. Of interest are the following comments from the psychological evaluations:

> The behavior of ... Laura and Shelley, reflects the problems that these two teenagers were experiencing at home with both their physical environment and their relationship with their parents. In addition to having to climb over piles of junk to move around their home, there must have been a significant level of embarrassment about not being able to invite anyone to their home. There was also the issue that if the authorities ever found [out] about the condition of their home, that the two daughters would most certainly be removed from their home and placed in protective custody ... The acting-out behavior of both girls (running away from home, drug use, and sexual promiscuity) was symptomatic of the problems at home that both daughters were experiencing." *Id.* at 327.

There was also evidence in the case that Laura "was sexually assaulted in February 1997 and did not tell her mother of the assault until sometime in April 1997; the minor did not report the sexual assault to the police or receive counseling as she was embarrassed and ashamed by the sexual assault; the minor and her mother were afraid the police would see the house." *Id.* at 326.

"...the minor did not report the sexual assault to the police or receive counseling as she was embarrassed and ashamed by the sexual assault; the minor and her mother were afraid the police would see the house."

Based upon the record, the appellate court affirmed the order that Shelley was a dependent child under the emotional abuse portions of the statute. The court found that a psychologist's opinion that Shelley was "suffering severe anxiety, depression, withdrawal, or untoward aggressive behavior toward herself or others" and that this emotional damage was due to the "deplorable unhealthy, unsafe, and embarrassing home conditions created by appellant and her husband" was adequate evidence to support the lower court's determination. *Id.* at 330.

Inappropriate conditions in a home have particular pertinence for adolescents. As teens are socialized and integrated into the community, there is an interaction between the home and the community that is natural and necessary. In high school my mother forbade me to visit one of my school friends. At the time I was unsure of the reason. As an adult I found that the father of this girl was a bootlegger in our "dry" county, and men were often coming into the home to buy whiskey. In addition, my friend's father was often seen in public in a drunken condition. It was an unsafe situation, and it impaired the teenage girl's ability to develop friendships and activities with other adolescents.

When a child's mother or father attempts to sexually entice a date or friend or engages in sexually explicit talk in the presence of children visiting in the home, the child will be most likely be cut off from the relationships necessary to develop appropriately.

When a child's mother or father attempts to sexually entice a date or friend or engages in sexually explicit talk in the presence of children visiting in the home, the child will be most likely be cut off from the relationships necessary to develop appropriately. This type of environment becomes a type of omission on the part of the parent because it isolates the children from others in the community. Unsafe or what the court called "embarrassing" homes constitute an emotional detriment for children that must evaluated.

Rejection occurs when a child hears such comments as, "Well, if you don't like it, you can get out." Similarly, "If you don't get your act together, I'll have you put in a home, and you'll never get out."

Chapter Twelve

Operational Definitions: Rejecting

DEFINITION

The parent consistently singles out one child to criticize and punish, to perform most of the household chores and to receive fewer rewards.

Possible Parental Behaviors

The child is frequently called derogatory, offensive and obscene names and also told that he/she is worthless or unwanted. The parent blames the child for most, if not all, domestic and financial problems. The child is shamed or humiliated, especially in the presence of peers, and is also ridiculed for displaying normal emotions. The parent routinely requires the child to eat all meals in isolation or seclusion from the family or at a different time.

Implications

In diagnosing family interaction over the years, the child who was the object of these behaviors was often referred to as a scapegoat child. In this respect the parent rejects the child as a person, finding scathing fault, heaping the worst chores on this child, and holding him or her responsible for everything that goes wrong. "It's your fault that your daddy left." "It's your fault I lost my job." "It's your fault that we had to move." "If it weren't for you, we would all be better off."

"Children who have been psychologically rejected by their parents or other primary caregivers are hostile and aggressive, have impaired self-esteem, and show excessive dependency on parents." Children who are rejected "see themselves as having few strengths and skills [and] view the world as hostile and unwilling to assist them." (Monteleone, 1996)

In addition, this rejection results in overt isolation of the child by not including him in special activities, not buying him or her treats that the other children receive, or forcing him to eat in his room or the back porch. This may be accompanied by a statement such as, "You don't deserve to be with the rest of us." In many cases the other children are allowed to mistreat, verbally abuse, or punish this child.

Perhaps the most damaging of these behaviors involves ridiculing a child for showing normal emotions. A child needs to be able to share emotions and understand his/her own emotions as well as the emotions of others. Parents who ridicule normal emotions thwart and ultimately may destroy the child's ability to deal with his/her emotions in a healthy manner. The chance of being taunted for crying, feeling hurt, or being afraid not only denies the child the opportunity to learn about his/her own feelings, but means a child will not see the parent demonstrate the critical element of empathy. Feelings that should be normal and accepted become a weapon that can be used against the child.

Feelings that should be normal and accepted become a weapon that can be used against the child.

As a result of this emotional abuse, the child frequently has difficulty in communicating. O'Hagen states that the child who has experienced this type of abuse is dominated by "negative emotion" or the repression of all emotion. "[T]he emotionally abused child who has learnt to adapt to or survive the abuse by expressing as little emotion as possible, or by expressing negative emotion predominantly, will have severe communication difficulties." (O'Hagan, 1993)

The child who is punished, ostracized or ridiculed for showing normal emotions will shut these emotions down or substitute negative or inappropriate responses that will in turn trigger even more punishment or ridicule. Such children are often unable to integrate socially in an acceptable way or develop relationships normally. The result from this type of emotional abuse is not immediately apparent or easily connected to the cause. When a child is quiet or unresponsive, many adults in the child's life are relieved and unconcerned.

The child who is punished, ostracized or ridiculed for showing normal emotions will shut these emotions down or substitute negative or inappropriate responses that will in turn trigger even more punishment or ridicule.

Rejecting behaviors were the subject of attention in *State v. Stevens,* 797 P.2d 1133 (Utah Ct. App. 1990). In that case, the appellate court affirmed the termination of a father's parental rights as to his daughter. There were several children in the family. The mother of the child in question had died soon after childbirth, and her father had remarried. Both parents had children from other marriages and a child of their own. The actions of the stepmother toward the child had brought the situation to the attention of CPS. There were some allegations of physical abuse by the stepmother, but there was also evidence of this cluster of abusive behaviors to CPS by the child's siblings: requiring the child "to spend long periods of time in her room and to retire to bed three hours before the other children" and

> incidents of Deanna [stepmother] clamping a wooden clothes pin over L.D.S.'s lips, locking L.D.S. in the back of a station wagon on a hot summer day, slapping L.D.S. when she did not eat properly, assigning L.D.S. a disproportionate amount of

> household tasks, displaying favoritism to the other children, forcefully spanking and kicking L.D.S., keeping L.D.S. in her room for most of the day, and not allowing L.D.S. to talk at the dinner table. *Id.* at 1136.

Upon evaluation, a psychiatrist determined that the symptoms of the child "fit the clinical picture of a neglected, mistreated, and emotionally abused child."

The father contended that termination of his rights was inappropriate since the stepmother had carried out the abuse. The lower court found, and the appellate court agreed, that termination was appropriate because the father was aware of his wife's conduct toward his daughter, and he had refused or failed to properly care for and protect his child. *Id.* at 1139.

It is important to note that, when this family and the treatment of the child were first brought to the attention of CPS, the father "admitted to a social worker that his wife, Deanna, prohibited him and other family members from touching L.D.S., explaining that it was Deanna's solution to avoid making a baby of L.D.S." *Id.* at 1135. The first investigation was closed when insufficient evidence of child abuse was discovered. The reports continued over the next two years and included "assertions that L.D.S. had multiple bruises; was never seen playing outside with the other children; appeared emotionally starved, hollow-eyes, apathetic, unresponsive, and withdrawn; and was often dressed inappropriately." *Id.* Eventually, after these multiple reports accumulated, the evidence and the findings of mental health professionals led to a successful termination proceeding. In the meantime, her caretakers exposed the child to years of emotionally damaging behavior.

The court also reacted to ostracism and rejection in *In Interest of E.B.L.* 501 N.W.2d 547 (Iowa 1993), where a mother appealed the termination of her rights to two of her children. She had seven children. The father of her six oldest children had sexually abused at least three of them, and his rights had already been terminated. The

State filed a termination petition as to the mother with regard to the six children. She consented to termination of her rights to the two youngest of her children by him.

The lower court ordered the return to the mother of the two oldest children and termination of the two middle children. This particular case was the mother's second appeal of the termination order. The Supreme Court of Iowa affirmed the termination. The Court noted that both children suffered serious mental and emotional harm from "the actions of their father and inaction of their mother ... During supervised visits there was little interaction between [the chil dren] and their mother. [The son] is made the scapegoat by his mother and she attempts to turn the other children again him." *Id.* at 550. The Supreme Court found that termination was appropriate because the mother did not have the parenting skills and ability to deal with the emotional damage done to these two children.

Perhaps the most interesting aspect of the opinion was the reference to "actions of their father and inaction of their mother." The court accurately assessed the damage of the overt act of emotional abuse as well as the passive act of emotional neglect or failure to act.

DEFINITION

The parent has unrealistic expectations of achievement for the child and criticizes, punishes, ostracizes or condemns the child when he/she does not achieve far above his/her normal abilities in areas such as school, arts, sports or social status.

Possible Parental Behaviors

The parent typically responds to the child's accomplishments with denigration or criticism, comparing him/her unfavorably and/or critically to adult performance. Praise, support, or recognition for improved skills is typically not given. The parent often tells the child that he/she is a failure.

Implications

This is the child who is rejected because the standards set by the parent are too high to be achieved. There is no way he can measure up, and, therefore, he can never achieve approval. In addition to the rejection aspect, there is also a chance that the child feels terror knowing that no matter what he does, it will be wrong, and punishment or rejection will surely follow. This child is under duress most of the time, and he/she can react either by not trying at all, resulting in inertia, or by feverishly attempting to fulfill expectations that are beyond his/her ability, resulting in obsessive behaviors and stress. Either way he cannot win.

...there is also a chance that the child feels terror knowing that no matter what he does, it will be wrong, and punishment or rejection will surely follow.

These parental behaviors erode two very important parts of a child's internal compass—hope and optimism. Daniel Goleman says that, "... having hope means that one will not give in to overwhelming anxiety, a defeatist attitude, or depression in the face of difficult challenges or setbacks." Students with a high level of hope, according to Goleman, worked harder in school and thought of ways they could improve their grades. Students with little hope gave up, demoralized. Optimism is a partner to hope. It is an attitude that buffers people against falling into apathy, hopelessness or depression in the face of tough going. (Goleman, 1995) The presence of optimism and hope allows a child to pick up and keep going, and represents the all-important characteristic of resiliency.

When parental behaviors do not encourage hope and optimism, and actually negate or deplete these internal strengths, the child cannot be expected to acquire the emotionally healthy elements of confidence and curiosity. When there is no value placed on progress or even minimal improvement, then there is no room for hope and no reason to try.

Certainly it is possible for parents to set high standards for their children and still make the child feel valued and loved. However, parents who do not accompany high expectations with affection, confirmation, and acceptance place so much stress on a child that he/she feels worthless, discouraged, and inferior. The child believes that lack of achievement is a personal indictment of self-worth. These feelings of failure foster the child's sense that his real value is based on performance instead of basic, inherent self-worth. Monteleone states that these children are more vulnerable to stress related illnesses, eating disorders, suicide and depression. (Monteleone, 1996)

Certainly it is possible for parents to set high standards for their children and still make the child feel valued and loved.

The *New York Times* reported a mother who claimed prodigious feats of genius for her eight-year-old son (March 12, 2002, "The Uneasy Fit of the Precocious and the Average Child," by Erica Goode). She falsified records and helped him cheat on intelligence tests. She claimed he played the violin at age 2 and competitive chess at age three. At the time the article was written, however, he was in foster care. He had been placed there after he became suicidal and had to be hospitalized. At a hearing, the mother admitted that she had created an "injurious environment" for her child.

DEFINITION

The parent confuses the child's sexual identity.

Possible Parental Behaviors

The parent forces the child to dress in clothing that is inappropriate for both sex and age, resulting in social ostracism. The parent frequently addresses, refers to, defines, or teases the child as if he/she is a member of the opposite sex.

Implications

This behavior is seen in a parent who views this as a perfectly acceptable way to discipline a child. With no knowledge or regard for the fact that gender is an extremely tender, vulnerable spot for a child, the parent may seek to punish his son by forcing him to wear a dress stating, "If you are going to act like a girl, we'll dress you like one." There is most likely a desire to demean, put down, and ridicule the child using gender as a basis. Most of this behavior is directed toward boys since having any feminine characteristics is considered weak and inferior in many families.

There is most likely a desire to demean, put down, and ridicule the child using gender as a basis.

The father/son relationship where this is most likely to occur is where competition and criticism become the father's approach to parenting a son whom he sees as a threat to him for dominance. He resorts to many tactics to hold on to the position of power in the family. The father's lack of understanding of his own emotions as well as those of his son can lead to inappropriate parenting behavior.

The hazing behavior that results may involve gender harassment, for the father remembers similar experiences as a child and sees it as male right of passage. Statements about penis size, body mass, facial hair and other gender-related barbs are an adult male's attempt to compete for dominance. The father may see this as just fun, like verbal scuffling; the boy sees it differently. "There is an inevitable conflict between the growing confidence and power of the adolescent and the increasingly defensive posture of the father." (Kindlon & Thompson, 1999). The father reaches for the tool that he knows will hurt and questions the boy's masculinity.

As a result of hazing, ridicule, and pressure to appear masculine, these boys must reject anything remotely unmanly. "[T]hey consciously and deliberately attack in others and in themselves traits that might possibly be defined as feminine. This includes tenderness, empathy, compassion, and any show of emotional vulnerability." (Kindlon & Thompson, 1999) Although sometimes mild, the use of gender and gender identification as a weapon to harm has long been a part of some families' treatment of children. This type of teasing or taunting is present in families where an emphasis is placed on being "macho." It may be perceived as a rite of passage for a boy and a necessary part of growing up. However, just because this is prevalent and somewhat institutionalized does not mean it cannot be extremely harmful to a child.

Although sometimes mild, the use of gender and gender identification as a weapon to harm has long been a part of some families' treatment of children.

This type of gender or sexual taunting by a father was the basis for granting a petition filed by CPS that a boy was an abused child in *Matter of Shane T., supra*. The record showed that the boy "has been repeatedly called a 'fag', 'faggot', and 'queer' by his natural father ..." His father had taunted him continually, publicly and privately, by saying that he should have been a girl. As we have previously noted, in New York the term "risk to emotional health" is defined only within a physical injury. Here, the Court found that a "physical injury" did not have to be inflicted by physical force and that it "encompasses the stomach pain experienced by Shane when his father challenged the boy's sexual identity." *Id.* at 591. The Court went on to note that:

> Thus, it is sufficient for a finding of abuse that there be protracted impairment of emotional health or a substantial risk thereof. It is clear, therefore, that it is the actual or potential impact on the child, as opposed to the per se seriousness of the injury, that forms the predicate for abuse.... [T]o constitute abuse, mere

> words are sufficient provided that their effect on the child falls within the language of the statute, To hold otherwise would constitute an unjustifiably narrow interpretation of the statute that would frustrate the legislature's intent. *Id.* at 593.

The fact that Shane suffered stomach aches arising from the abuse was adequate for the Court to find that he had suffered "physical injury" from to his father's verbal abuse. The Court went on to say: "The behavior of this respondent father is as serious a form of abuse as if he had plunged a knife into the stomach of this child. In fact, it's probably worse since the agony and heartache suffered by Shane has already assailed him for several years and constitutes a grave and imminent threat to his future psychological development." *Id.* at 594.

Finally, the Court also found that the boy was an abused child with respect to his mother. The Court noted that she had been unable to protect the boy from the abusive behavior of his father and approved the removal of the boy from the custody of both parents. As seen in other cases, active abusive behavior and a passive omission or failure to protect combined to create an environment that was unacceptable for a child.

DEFINITION

The parent provides no stability or security for the child.

Possible Parental Behaviors

Expectations are unpredictable and change frequently, resulting in requirements for the child that range from rigid at one time to indifference to behavioral standards later. The parent regularly encourages or tells the child to leave home, threatens to expel the child, to send him/her to a "home" or to have the child "locked up." The parent refuses to listen to the child's position and does not protect the child from unwarranted criticism or abuse from others. The parent regularly lies to the child about the other parent, relatives or siblings.

Implications

If the bedrock of security is predictability, as many people feel, then this set of parental behaviors is its antithesis. A combination of *rejection*, *terrorizing*, and perhaps *corrupting*, these behaviors attack the very core of a child's trust, balance, and sense of safety.

The child who experiences these behaviors has no map to use to chart his/her own behavior, because the person who holds the map keeps changing the lines and parameters.

The child who experiences these behaviors has no map to use to chart his/her own behavior, because the person who holds the map keeps changing the lines and parameters. One day it is all right to fix a snack after school; the next day, it may be a serious offense. This is a type of psychological warfare where the parent places the child in a state of constant wariness, wondering what to do to please the parent. In some ways it is like playing football on a field with no lines. One doesn't know when he/she is out of bounds, has scored a touchdown, or made a first down until someone blows a whistle. The uncertainty is always present.

Considering that children need to know the rules and the boundaries, the lack of established rules creates a state of chaos and flux. When I was ordered by a judge to pick up two children from school one day and place them in foster care, I remember that the older girl looked up at me and said, "Lady, just tell me how it's going to be. I think I can get used to it if you will tell me how it is going to be." Her statement reflected a need to hear from an adult what she could expect in the future. The future for a child is day to day. All of us feel safer and more comfortable with a rhythm or routine in our lives. Many of the material deficits of life, such as not having meat every day or name brand clothes, are neutralized when there is a caring, nurturing family. This explains why children living in poverty can look back and say, "We didn't have anything but beans and cornbread, but mother and daddy loved us, and it was all right." Those children "knew how it was going to be."

Rejection occurs when a child hears such comments as, "Well, if you don't like it, you can get out."

Rejection occurs when a child hears such comments as, "Well, if you don't like it, you can get out." Similarly, "If you don't get your act together, I'll have you put in a home, and you'll never get out." The terrorizing comes with threats such as, "If you screw up again, I'm calling the police and having you put in reform school. Then you'll see who's boss." These constant threats to put the child out of the home, whether followed through or not, create a state of uncertainty and unrest. The question of whether a child deserves to be expelled or punished is really not the issue in many cases. Instead these behaviors are the parent's way of reminding the child who is in control and who has the power to act on these threats.

One of the most dangerous parts of this behavior cluster lies in the parent's failure to protect the child from others. Because of a lack of empathy for the child, and perhaps a lack of self-esteem themselves, the parent does not assume the role of protector or advocate for the child. Without a protector, the child is fair game and vulnerable to abuse, ridicule, and inappropriate treatment from other adults. These behaviors were some of those addressed by the court in *In Interest of N.N., supra*, a case previously discussed in the context of the passive parent being found to be responsible for emotional abuse. There, the father failed to protect his daughter from abuse at the hands of the mother. The court found that the mother had consistently and publicly degraded their daughter by consistently calling her names like "slut" and "whore." The father had not prevented the abuse.

This lack of protection sets the stage for boyfriends or girlfriends of the parent, friends of the family, or relatives to attack this child verbally. The child is defenseless. An uncle may say, "Look at you. You have no tits. Nobody's going to want you." No one says a word to help the child. A friend of the father's can say to a young boy, "You're such a girly-girly. Bet you don't even pee standing up." No one says a word. Often the parent will join in the ridicule or hazing.

There is also a danger or potential for sexual abuse of a child who does not have a parent to protect him/her. People visiting in the home, temporarily living in the home, or held in esteem by the parent are allowed to make sexually explicit remarks, or permitted to walk up behind a fourteen year old girl washing dishes, place hands on her breasts and fondle her. No one will intervene.

There is also a danger or potential for sexual abuse of a child who does not have a parent to protect him/her.

These behaviors are reinforced because of another facet of this cluster. The parent does not give the child an opportunity to explain his/her side of any problem or disagreement and does not give any credence to what the child may say. It is not unusual to hear such statements such as, "Just shut up. I know it's your fault. You're always getting into trouble, and I don't want to hear one word you have to say."

Finally, this child has no security because the parent lies about the other people in his/her life who are important. The parent misrepresents the feelings and opinions of other important family members to the child, using this information to criticize and hurt. "Your mother doesn't care a whit about you. Why should she?", is a hurtful comment that may or may not have any truth in it. "Your brother said you were a loser, and I agree with him." The parent uses the child's love for others as a lever to hurt and control.

Many of these parental behaviors were implicated in *In Interest of C.N.T.*, 771 P.2d 561, 1989 Kan.App. LEXIS 159 (Kan.Ct.App. 1989). (The Memorandum Opinion in this case was not designated for publication and was a *per curiam* affirmation of the lower court's termination of parental rights to a couple's four minor children.) The evidence before the lower court revealed that both parents had varying mental illnesses that had severely impacted each of their children. Various professionals testified as to the following types of emotional abuse and neglect:

Father allowed his brother to put his hands in the children's pants and told a child not to tell the mother that the brother had been found on top of one of the children…

Emotional abuse: Father allowed his brother to put his hands in the children's pants and told a child not to tell the mother that the brother had been found on top of one of the children; the children were continually exposed to the father's hostility toward his wife and "specifically … continued the turmoil with his wife to the point where the children were severely impaired emotionally and developmentally." The mother blamed one of the children for the things that his siblings did. 1989 Kan.App. LEXIS at 8.

Emotional neglect: While the children were at their father's, the children were "out of control, wild, and did not have limits placed upon them." One mental health professional testified that the children "were reminiscent of feral children, which are children who grow up without any human contact." A caseworker stated that, while at the mother's "the children were allowed to do what they wanted to do and there appeared to be no type of structure. The children were hungry and not given enough food when with the mother and were allowed outside inappropriately dressed during cold weather." *Id.* at 9.

The lower court had testimony that there was an inability on the part of each parent to adjust his/her conduct "to meet the needs of the children, especially their continued hostility toward each other and the use of the children as pawns in connection therewith" and that "neither parent has been able to put aside his or her own needs in favor of the children." *Id.* at 10.

> there was an inability on the part of each parent to adjust his/her conduct "to meet the needs of the children, especially their continued hostility toward each other and the use of the children as pawns in connection therewith"

Mental health professionals concluded that the children "were severely impaired emotionally and developmentally." Since improvement in the situation was not likely to occur regardless of the extent of services provided to them, the lower court terminated the parental rights. The appellate court affirmed this determination.

Another case involving a chaotic environment was addressed in *State in Interest of Four Minor Children v. D.W., 585 So.2d 1222* (La.Ct.App. 2 Cir. 1991) where a mother appealed the termination of parental rights to her four children. The children of D.W. had initially come to the attention of CPS because of allegations of physical abuse. On investigation and evaluation, however, each of the children was found to have signs of severe emotional abuse. *Id.* at 1225. A psychologist's evaluation of the mother "confirmed her abusive personality, reflecting D.W.'s strong interest and concern for her own needs, suspicious pattern of behavior, and difficulty maintaining effort and energy for everyday tasks. He found D.W. has a tendency to involve herself in highly emotional situations, but has difficulty keeping her behavior within limits and controls, with a high degree of variability in her behavior." *Id.* The three oldest of D.W.'s children were found to be "experiencing a high level of emotional conflict, fear of D.W., resentment, and anxiety. Generally, the psychological evaluations ... reflect severe conflict and disturbance in the home resulted in the children's emotional and medical needs not being met." *Id.* at 1226. The termination order was affirmed.

A contrary result was reached in a case because of the heightened evidentiary burden imposed by the Indian Child Welfare Act. As noted previously, the ICWA imposes a standard of beyond a reasonable doubt for termination of parental rights where a case involves a Native American. This standard was applicable *In re: Jessica T.,* 1993 Conn.Super. LEXIS 3480 (Conn. Super. Ct. Dec. 20, 1993) (unreported opinion) because Jessica's mother was one-half Alaskan Native American. In ruling on a petition to terminate the mother's rights filed by the Department of Children and Youth Services, there were opinions by many experts that it would be in Jessica's best interests to have her mother's rights terminated. All of the experts who evaluated the mother and child noted that the mother displayed a lack of empathy toward her daughter and would blame the child for all of the problems between them. The mother viewed Jessica as "spoiled" and manipulative and interacted with the child always in a negative manner. The position of the evaluators was that the mother "has not acknowledged abuse of the child, is 'too laid-back' in her parenting style, exhibits an inability to praise her daughter, and places blame on Jessica for any incompatibility within the family unit. Petitioner (as well as counsel for the child) urges termination of the mother's parental rights, not on the basis of recurring physical abuse, but upon likely emotional damage to the child if returned to the mother's care...." *Id.* at 83.

Despite this expert testimony, the trial court dismissed the petition stating:

> [The mother] was reared exclusively by one parent, her mother (the maternal grandmother), who was a full blooded Alaskan Indian. The likely influence of such upbringing and heritage is, in the court's view, reinforced by evidence that much in the mother's

parenting style, which the psychologists considered so problematic, is described as "culturally normative"... ; that is, what has been characterized in these proceedings as laid-back parenting, allowing too much freedom, insufficient setting and maintaining of limits, overpermissive, non-interference, resort to shame and ridicule, etc. *Id.* at 88-89.

Unlike civil or criminal cases where precedential case law shapes current applications and findings, family court law moves along with research and best practice.

The court criticized the therapy offered to the mother as not taking into account her cultural background, and accordingly, refused to find "beyond a reasonable doubt" that the parental rights of the mother should be terminated.

This case was brought over ten years ago. There is no doubt that family courts can shift and modify their approach to child welfare issues. Unlike civil or criminal cases where precedential case law shapes current applications and findings, family court law moves along with research and best practice. For that reason, policy changes that reflect the basis for expert opinions brought to the attention of the court may change and affect outcome.

DEFINITION

The parent does not permit the child autonomy or independent learning.

Possible Parental Behaviors

The parent becomes angry, insulting and/or critical toward the child if he or she expresses any individual thoughts or opinions or has feelings about situations or people that are different from the parent's. The parent consistently tells and threatens the child that if he or she tries to make decisions independently of the parent, or is too curious, then terrifying consequences, possibly death, will happen to the child. The parent always speaks for the child and does not permit any independent expression or treat the child as a separate person with his or her own concerns.

Implications

This set of behaviors is an example of extreme intrusion, where the parent seeks to control the child by making all of the decisions involving the child's activities or circumstances. In an extreme situation, this is a form of mind control where the child is not allowed the independence to make choices that are appropriate for his age and maturity and necessary for his psycho/social development. The parent's intent in these behaviors may vary. The parent may have such a need to control what the child thinks and believes that he or she is afraid to allow the child to explore ideas that are different. This fear may come from a philosophical or religious framework where the parent wishes to ensure that the child adheres to those positions. A part of this fear may be a concern that the "outside world" will have an adverse or corrupting influence on the child.

Another reason for this behavior is simply the parent's need for power. In this case, the parent attempts to dominate by not allowing the child to have any control or power in the relationship. The parent may choose the toys the child plays with, the friends they have, the clothes they wear, and other choices that are more appropriately left to the child as the child is able to handle them. We would agree that a parent needs to be involved in the choices a child makes; however, the developmental process requires an increasing range of decision-making situations where children can exert their own personality and learn from the consequences of their choices.

Within a healthy family unit, the child learns to "engage others and be understood," which is what Goleman calls relatedness. It is in this context that the child learns to form, express and share opinions and ideas on a variety of subjects. Given the opportunity, the child will approach the parent with an idea or opinion on such subjects as politics, school rules, religion or other subjects for discussion. The child needs to be able to express the opinion, or even take an oppositional position, in order to evoke a discussion. Perhaps in adolescence it is a more common occurrence for the discussion to be provocative; however, this also is part of the learning process. It is not necessary for the parent to agree for there to be productive conversation. Without such dialogue, the child is left to form opinions based on input or feedback primarily from friends or television. In families where there are emotionally abusive behaviors, a child is unable to express himself for fear that he will be rejected, ostracized, or at the very least, ridiculed, for his opinions or feelings.

In families where there are emotionally abusive behaviors, a child is unable to express himself for fear that he will be rejected, ostracized, or at the very least, ridiculed, for his opinions or feelings.

A case describing inappropriate intrusion into the life of child that caused emotional harm is *Jackson v. W., supra*. There, after hearing evidence, the hearing officer upheld the Department's "founded disposition of emotional abuse" with the following comment: "It is determined that requiring a six-year-old child to use a bottle in spite of [protest], requiring that the six-year-old child shower with [his father] and the insistence of wiping and cleaning the six-year-old child after he uses the bathroom, are clear and convincing [evidence] of 'behaviors which are considered intimidating, humiliating ... or excessively guilt-producing ....'" 419 S.E.2d at 396.

This parent's compulsive behaviors, whether realized or not, represented an intrusion or control that cannot be justified. The parent apparently saw his behavior as necessary to satisfy his (the parent's) need for hygiene. Because of his own needs, the father was unable to grasp the damage of his intrusion, all but negating the possibility for change. Once again, it is clear that the intent of the parent who engages in damaging behaviors cannot be the basis for intervening on behalf of a child.

DEFINITION

The parent regularly denigrates and ridicules the child, stating without foundation, that he or she is different, in many undesirable ways, from others in the household or reminds everyone of a person who is totally offensive and unacceptable by the family.

Possible Parental Behaviors

Although innocent, the parent frequently calls the child names, such as "liar", "thief", or "whore", and regularly tells the child that he or she is physically unacceptable, such as too fat, too thin or uncoordinated. The parent also humiliates or ridicules the child in the presence of the child's peers. The child is shamed for showing normal emotions, such as affection, grief or sorrow.

Implications

These behaviors generally reflect a lack of empathy on the parent's part. Unable to feel the pain or humiliation of the child, there is no governor on the parent's behavior. The name-calling that follows becomes a routine of rejection. When the parent lacks the ability to get outside his or her own skin and feel what the child feels, then the parent is unable to set limits on his own hurtful behaviors. This lack of empathy, or being able to see the child's perspective, may also be an impetus for physical abuse as well.

Since empathy is developed in children primarily birth to five, a parent who did not develop an ability to feel for others is actually unable to give this to a child.

Without the restraint provided by the presence of empathy, the parent attacks the child verbally. The validity of the accusation is irrelevant. Whether the child is innocent or guilty, the extreme response of the parent is, at the very least, destructive to the child's self-concept and trust in the parent. Name-calling, for whatever reason, is negative and teaches the child nothing, except how to call other people names.

Despite the seriousness of verbal assaults, the most destructive of these parental behaviors may be the parent's refusing to allow the child to respond normally to pain or hurt. We have a parent who is not only willing to hurt the child's feelings, but will not allow the child to cry or be sad as a result of the hurt. This is a double injury for the child and the long-term implications are great. For a child to develop emotionally, he or she must be able to understand his or her own feelings and the feelings of others. When the parent refuses to allow the child to show emotions, this impairs the child's ability to develop this capacity. The child cannot develop empathy because that involves an understanding of one's own feeling and an appreciation for the feelings of others.

Despite the seriousness of verbal assaults, the most destructive of these parental behaviors may be the parent's refusing to allow the child to respond normally to pain or hurt.

The parent who verbally attacks a child, sees the child begin to cry, and says, "I'll give you something to cry about," has already given the child much to cry about. However, the greater damage to a child may come from not seeing the parent respond appropriately to his pain. Children who experience this rejection and psychological assault by parents often become hostile and aggressive. Ironically, the child can develop an unhealthy dependence on the parents, seeking to win the parents' favor and, therefore, avoid the rejection. This is sometimes referred to as "defensive independence" (Monteleone, 1996). This is the child who mistrusts those outside the family and has a generally negative attitude about the world. With a lack of self-esteem, this child obviously sees himself as having few desirable characteristics or skills.

A parent's lack of empathy was part of the evidence in a petition to terminate a father's rights in *In re M.W.,* 1998 Minn.App. LEXIS 1167 (Minn. Ct. App. Oct. 20, 1998) (an unreported opinion). The father requested custody of his children who had been removed from the home while he was hospitalized with a work injury. The mother consented to termination of her rights. At the time of his request, the family had been receiving services for six years, having come to the attention of the department because of abuse and neglect issues. The house had been found to be extremely dirty with rabbit feces and garbage. At the time the children entered foster care (ages then four to six) none were toilet trained. The children often went without food and were locked in their room by the mother who would cover the windows with blankets. All of the children were extremely emotionally damaged when they were evaluated upon entering foster care.

The following was noted by the court about the father's interactions with the children after their removal:

> Father's inability to care for his children was apparent at his visits with the children. His behavior was inappropriate, and he failed to follow through with staff recommendations. Father's behavior included kicking the children's cards, removing toys and snacks to make them cry, calling names, knocking over toys, and laughing when these actions made them cry. He displayed competitive behavior with the children. He talked negatively to them, withdrew attention, showed a disparate amount of attention to

> one child over another, and refused to acknowledge them when they required affection.
>
> The pervasiveness of emotional abuse and lack of any improvement by the father continued. Eventually, the guardian *ad litem* and the children's psychologist recommended termination of parental rights. *Id.* at 4-5.

The appellate court agreed with the determination of the lower court to terminate the father's rights, finding that the father was "palpably unfit to be a party to the parent and child relationship." *Id.* at 8.

This case demonstrates the court's reaction to an absence of empathy on the part of this father. His inability to feel the pain of his child is not only harmful to the child, but prevents his being able to offer any protection to this child from the assaults of others.

In an emotionally unhealthy parent/child relationship, the parent seeks to control the child through threats of harm. Whether or not the threat is actually carried out, the child knows that it is possible.

CHAPTER THIRTEEN

Operational Definitions: Terrorizing

DEFINITION

The parent uses excessive threats and psychological punishments.

Possible Parental Behaviors

For a variety of reasons, the parent threatens to desert the child, to remove needed and treasured possessions without promise of return, and threatens mutilation or dismemberment. Punishments include exposure to acutely fearful situations, verbal assaults and taunts by household members, prolonged isolation, and the prohibition of household members' communication with the child.

Implications

This set of behaviors is a primary example of the emotionally abusive category of terrorizing. Because of the disparity of power between the parent and the child, these types of behaviors represent more than just threats to the child. The child feels that the parent is capable of following through on the threats. In other words, what a normal person might see as a ridiculous, hollow threat, the child sees as reality.

Terrorizing or psychological abuse is a type of treatment seen through the years in prisoner of war camps. The POW is at the total mercy of his captor; he knows that anything is possible. When the captor makes a threat involving any sort of punishment, torture or brutality, the prisoner is manipulated through his own fear of what is possible. In an emotionally unhealthy parent/child relationship, the parent seeks to control the child through threats of harm. Whether or not the threat is actually carried out, the child knows that it is possible. His fear is real and justified.

The absence of restraint on the part of the parent demonstrates a complete lack of empathy for the child. Instead, we see an overt desire to harm. Parents who use terrorizing as a means of discipline may say, "When you come home from school today, we'll all be gone and you will never find us." The parent can threaten the child by saying, "While you're at school, I'm going to take your dog to the pound and have it put to sleep." These are examples of how a non-empathetic parent locates a tender spot in the child, such as his concern for a pet or special toy and uses this against the child. If one person knows what another holds dear, this may become a source of power and control.

In extreme cases, the parent will hold the child's hand over boiling water, telling him what will happen if he doesn't carry out the parent's wishes.

In extreme cases, the parent will hold the child's hand over boiling water, telling him what will happen if he doesn't carry out the parent's wishes. The parent makes other threats, such as holding the child out of a second or third story window, opening the car door at high speeds while threatening to throw the child out or telling the child he will cut his fingers off one at a time. In a relationship such as this, the child has often witnessed the erratic and unpredictable behavior of the parent and senses that there is no real limitation on the things that the parent might be willing to do. The child is already fearful about his safety. The parent has never acted as a protector so it is easy to see why the child believes this could actually happen.

The child not only has to fear the threatened harm; he may also fear even more extreme consequences.

A number of years ago, I had placed Gina, a seriously abused eleven year old, in a residential treatment center in a nearby city. Her self-destructive behaviors had become so serious that she required in-patient treatment. One weekend a month, I would drive two hours to pick her up for a visit to her foster parents. We were driving on the interstate at seventy miles per hour when she reached over and pulled open the door of the car. Frightened for her safety and mine, I quickly brought the car to a halt on shoulder of the road. When I turned to look at her, she appeared to be in a trance, staring off into space. After a few seconds, she said, "He used to hold me over the fire and tell me he would burn me up. He didn't do it, but I knew he could've."

..."He used to hold me over the fire and tell me he would burn me up. He didn't do it, but I knew he could've."

In this climate of uncertainty, the child is faced with a constant need to protect himself, to be watchful and to trust no one. All of his psychic energy goes into dealing with the unpredictability of the parent and trying to decide how to respond. It's no wonder this child cannot be successful in school or with peers because he can never relax long enough to think about routine activities that children normally enjoy. If parental behaviors are related to drug and/or alcohol abuse, for example, the child's behavior at school will mirror the pattern of the parent. Robbie, an eighth grader whose father would go on two-week drinking binges

In this climate of uncertainty, the child is faced with a constant need to protect himself, to be watchful and to trust no one.

during which he would abuse the entire family, would come to school and lay his head on his desk for the entire two weeks. The teacher knew the day the binge began and the day it ended by merely observing his behavior.

The child who is the victim of this type of emotional abuse may be withdrawn at school, appearing to be in a daze or disinterested. He may do enough work to get by, but he does not connect or otherwise engage with the teacher or the other students. The quiet child who causes no problems in the classroom may be easily overlooked and receive no special help or services. Notes on the permanent record may say such things as "underachiever," "spacey," "doesn't try" or "anti-social."

The child who is the victim of this type of emotional abuse may be withdrawn at school, appearing to be in a daze or disinterested.

In *State in Interest of Quilter,* 424 So.2d 394 (La.Ct.App. 2 Cir. 1982), the appellate court upheld orders of a lower court awarding custody of two minor daughters to the Department of Health and Human Resources, terminating their mother's visitation rights and ordering commencement of proceedings to terminate her parental rights. The lower court found that the two had been exposed to violent arguments between their mother and stepfather. "The young girls also became a frequent target of their mother's consuming hostility, and as such, they were the repeated subjects of verbal abuse and threats by their mother. Mrs. Aswell threatened her daughters with having their throats cut or returning to a

"The young girls also became a frequent target of their mother's consuming hostility, and as such, they were the repeated subjects of verbal abuse and threats by their mother...."

foster home. Mrs. Aswell admitted that she subjected her daughters to mental abuse by threatening them and by screaming at them." *Id.* at 396. The Louisiana appellate court found that: "The record clearly shows that Mrs. Aswell is incapable of meeting the emotional needs of her daughters. When in her care Christy and Angela are subjected to not only damaging neglect of their emotional needs but also to active emotional abuse." *Id.* at 399.

Psychological battering and terrorizing can be no less damaging than instances where individuals are captured, whether in war or as part of a kidnapping, subjected to constant threats of bodily harm and made to witness the abuse of others. The close relationship and attachment that the child feels for the parent intensifies the impact and the amount of damage done to the child's emotional development.

Psychological battering and terrorizing can be no less damaging than instances where individuals are captured, whether in war or as part of a kidnapping, subjected to constant threats of bodily harm and made to witness the abuse of others.

Parental corrupting behaviors teach and reinforce antisocial or deviant patterns that tend to make the child unable to function in a normal social setting.

Chapter Fourteen

Operational Definitions: Corrupting

DEFINITION

The parent exposes the child to maladaptive and harmful influences.

Possible Parental Behaviors

The parent engages in serious criminal activity with the full awareness of the child, also encouraging the child to steal, engage in illegal activities and to attack others. The parent forces the child to use marijuana and alcohol and to become "high" or intoxicated, all for the entertainment of the parent and his/her friends. The child is exposed to the parent's regular intoxication. The parent also forces the child to watch cruel behavior toward a family pet and encourages him/her to torment or abuse animals.

Implications

This cluster of parental behaviors is the essence of corrupting as a category of emotional maltreatment. Here we have the parent, who should set the standard for the family moral code, both modeling and fostering behaviors that are illegal or inhumane. The parent's actions themselves have a strong influence on the attitudes, behaviors, and values of the child; however, this cluster goes beyond the passive exposure to wrong to the active teaching of wrong. "Parental corrupting behaviors teach and reinforce antisocial or deviant patterns that tend to make the child unable to function in a normal social setting. In milder forms, the parents convey approval of or encourage the child's precocious interest and/or behavior in the area of sexuality, aggression, violence, or substance abuse." (Monteleone, 1996) These parents do not teach the basic tenet of respect for others and encourage the child to never trust others.

The child of this family may appear to be advanced in maturity; however, it is a pseudo-maturity not unlike we see in children who are sexually abused.

The child of this family may appear to be advanced in maturity; however, it is a pseudo-maturity not unlike we see in children who are sexually abused. They take on the false confidence, sometimes bravado, of the parent who teaches them to "get somebody before they get you." This results in behavior that is aggressive toward peers or animals, lacks compassion, and is not responsive to the needs of others. This parent is the one who says, "If you don't hit him back, I will beat you myself."

A colleague told me about a situation involving friends of her teenage daughter. There had been a disagreement between two ninth grade girls. When one of the girls went home and told her mother, the mother said, "Go back to that school tomorrow and beat her up. If you don't, you'll be in trouble with me." The following afternoon the mother stood outside the school to see that her daughter confronted and attacked the other child. The parent did not just advise, she forced the child to be physically aggressive in a manner that could result in arrest or suspension from school.

The abuse of drugs and/or alcohol in front of a child, for many years thought to be a non-issue or at least a low priority with CPS, is now seen in a different light. A parent who is drunk and passed out on the sofa is a parent who does not supervise the child or interact with the child to give stimulation and guidance.

She also models destructive behavior. Indeed, in *Doe v. Doe (In re Doe), supra*, a mother's habitual alcohol and drug addictions provided the basis for a termination of her rights to her daughter. The mother had initially been given primary physical custody of the child after a divorce. During the two years that this custody arrangement was in place, the mother regularly consumed alcohol and used illegal drugs in the presence of the child. Eventually, the father successfully obtained physical custody of the child. Due to the mother's continuing addictive behaviors, the father filed for termination of her parental rights. The lower court found that the child had been neglected and even emotionally abused due to her mother's addictions and that termination was in the best interests of the girl. The mother appealed.

The lower court found that the child had been neglected and even emotionally abused due to her mother's addictions and that termination was in the best interests of the girl.

On appeal, the Supreme Court of Idaho found the following from the evidence:

> During the time that Roe [mother] had the minor child in her physical custody, she changed residences seven different times and cohabitated with several male friends. She regularly consumed alcohol and illegal drugs and was found lying unconscious with the minor child upset and crying by her side in the early morning hours. One of her ex-live-in boyfriends testified that he often had to care of the minor child because Roe was either in bed or unwilling to take on the responsibilities herself. As a result of her own conduct, Roe's contact with the minor child was reduced to protect the interests of the minor child. There is substantial, competent

> evidence to support the trial court's finding of neglect. *Id.* at 1209

With respect to considering the effect of the mother's addictions on the child, the Supreme Court stated:

> It is important to note two things in this respect: First, we are dealing with the life [of] a young child, now only 8 years of age, and that child has already lived through six or more years of varying degrees of neglect, and at a very minimum, emotional abuse, due to the addictive behaviors of her mother. Second, the mother's efforts at recovery and stabilization in her life—both of which would be absolutely necessary were she to be considered a proper parent for [the minor child]—may take longer than the childhood [the minor child] has left……[T]he child's progress should not have to be delayed because of the mother's inability to cope with her own problems. *Id.* at 1208

Because of the evidence and the concern for the best interests of the child, the Supreme Court affirmed the termination of parental rights as to the mother.

Alcoholism was also the basis for termination of parental rights in *Interest of Cheatwood, supra*. There, caseworkers found the mother intoxicated and confused and found the child unclothed, ill, and unattended on numerous occasions. The mother contended that termination was not appropriate because there was no evidence that her son had suffered "substantial harm." The appellate court disagreed, stating that 'nothing in the statutory definition of 'neglect suggests that a child must suffer demonstrable harm before the parent-child relationship can be terminated. It if sufficient that the child 'lacks parental care necessary for his health, morals and well-being.' The termination statutes of this state exist not merely to alleviate harm but to prevent it." *Id.* at 1234.

Exposure to the chaos and crime deriving from a home where the mother was addicted to drugs was addressed in a termination proceeding in *In re: Carrie B,* 1990 Conn. Super.LEXIS 155 (Conn. Super. Ct. July 23, 1990) (an unreported decision). In that case, the child had already been adjudicated as a neglected child, having specialized needs and suffering emotional neglect. At the time of her initial removal from her mother's home, Carrie was found to be "depressed, lacking in self-esteem and withdrawn. She was eneuretic; and aggressive to others." *Id.* at 9. After a period during which CPS attempted to work with the drug-addicted mother to seek rehabilitation, a petition to terminate parental rights was filed. Various witnesses testified that the mother had allowed a boyfriend (also a drug user) to live in the house even though he physically abused the mother and verbally abused the child. On one occasion the mother was arrested for shoplifting (something she did regularly to obtain money for her habit) while her daughter was with her. The officer testified that Carrie spat at him as he was arresting her mother. The court stated: "In short, the child was forced to live in a chaotic, abusive, filthy, drug-ridden house. The [mother] has done nothing since the child was committed to correct the situation. Conversely, she has undertaken to introduce the child to the world of shoplifting." *Id.* at 13. Because of the many ways that the mother failed to protect the child, exposed her to corrupting behaviors and emotionally neglected her, the petition to terminate the mother's rights was granted.

DEFINITION

The parent sexually exploits the child by forcing or permitting the child to watch pornographic materials.

Possible Parental Behaviors

The parent performs sexual acts in the presence of the child and forces or permits the child to watch and/or photograph adults engaged in sexual intercourse.

Implications

Although some professionals may see these behaviors only within the realm of sexual abuse, they are also emotionally abusive and neglectful. Many people define sexual abuse as "sexual contact between a child and an adult." Others see sexual abuse as involving a wide range of activities that provide sexual gratification to an adult. These behaviors, although they do not involve direct physical contact with the child, place the child in a position of providing the adult with sexual gratification. These types of behaviors may include the following: disrobing, nudity, sharing sexually explicit materials, explicit "sex talk" directed toward the child and photography of adults and/or children with a sexual connotation.

None of the behaviors above involve the more commonly understood forms of sexual abuse such as intercourse, anal and/or oral sex or mutual masturbation. However, since any use of a child for sexual gratification of an adult is inappropriate, there is an emotionally destructive component to these behaviors. The child is placed in an adult's position and is seen as a sex object. This is counter to the normal emotional development of a child. The child is made aware of and involved in activities that children normally do not experience. While the child is involved in these activities, he or she is not developing in other areas appropriately. A child who is sexually stimulated and involved in adult sexual activities, whether directly or indirectly, is in a very different place from his peers. A nine-year-old boy is supposed to be worried about tadpoles, baseballs, and earthworms, not preoccupied with sexual intercourse.

However, since any use of a child for sexual gratification of an adult is inappropriate, there is an emotionally destructive component to these behaviors.

Another destructive aspect of this type of emotional abuse is the mimicking behavior that we see in young children, where the child goes to daycare and imitates the sex act. The child then is branded a pervert or a sexually aggressive child, all because the child is attempting to be like the adults he admires. Older children may also become sexually promiscuous and seek to find confirmation and acceptance from others through sexual means.

DEFINITION

The custodial parent undermines the child's attachment to the other parent by consistently refusing all legitimate opportunities or requests for visits between the child and the other parent, even when these are requested by the child.

Possible Parental Behaviors

Most custodial arrangements are the product of a divorce proceeding where the parties involved have been instructed by court order to respect a visitation plan. Although the plan may not have been mutually acceptable, the parents are bound by the arrangement until the plan is modified.

In situations where visitation triggers emotional maltreatment, one parent does not respect the court order and uses various means to ignore or circumvent it. The parent does not assure that the child is available for the planned visit, uses excuses such as a child's unsubstantiated illness or activities to avoid the visit, attempts to make the child feel guilty for going or wanting to go or feigns illness to make the child feel he or she is needed to care for the parent.

There is no genuine attempt on the part of the parent to make the visitation plan work smoothly. This may or may not be known to the child. The child may be told or may perceive that the other parent doesn't show up, doesn't care, or cancels. If the child asks to go, the parent or other family members show disapproval or entice the child to resist.

Implications

Assuming that there is no justified and substantiated reason to resist visitation, the parent who refuses to cooperate with the court order or attempts to circumvent the visit is, on some level, using the child to punish or manipulate the other parent. Issues related to child support, other compensation, or life styles are used for justification for the behavior. The best interests of the child are not primary. In the process of justifying the non-compliance, the parent frequently demeans or discounts the other parent, often to the child.

The child is the child of both parents and, all things being equal, feels allegiance to both. His identify, self-esteem, and self-image are all tied to and related to both parents. He generally wants to feel free to love both. However, the parent, whether intentionally or not, who forces the child to choose or seeks to cast the other parent in a negative light, is stating that one-half of the child is unacceptable.

However, the parent, whether intentionally or not, who forces the child to choose or seeks to cast the other parent in a negative light, is stating that one-half of the child is unacceptable.

These conflicts, subterfuges, and attacks place the child in an arena totally unacceptable for his emotional health. He is buffeted back and forth, subjected to adult conversations, and designated as the object of the conflict, all conditions that impede or impair his ability to deal with normal developmental tasks relating to his age.

Since divorce and bitter custody battles have become the order of the day, all of us must be sensitive to the effects of these conflicts on children. If parents are not satisfied with the custody status or visitation plan, they must petition the court for a modification or rehearing. Courts must be sensitive to the need to reduce or limit the emotional damage that is heaped on a child as a result of two parents who would rather cut a child in half than accommodate the other parent. Perhaps the volume of cases and the grayness of the circumstances prevent appropriate redress. However, children are at stake in the process.

> Courts must be sensitive to the need to reduce or limit the emotional damage that is heaped on a child as a result of two parents who would rather cut a child in half than accommodate the other parent.

In *Pilger v. Pilger,* 972 S.W.2d 628 (Mo.Ct.App. 1998), the lower court addressed a visitation issue following a divorce. The trial court awarded custody to the mother and placed restrictions on the father's visitation rights "under such supervision and conditions as the mother determines that the children will be safe." The father appealed, contending that the visitation order was unenforceably vague. The father also contended that the trial court erred in allowing a psychologist to testify who had treated him as a patient. At the trial, the mother testified that the children said their father told them that their mother was doing drugs and using alcohol, was watching dirty movies, "that I was going, I was in the bathtub with men. That in the night I would sneak men in through the bedroom door. I was leaving them alone, that I was planning a trip to leave them and go to Colorado. Oh, a lot of, a lot of horrible, horrible lies. Cocaine, that I was doing cocaine…." *Id.* at 630. Additionally, the father had taken the children for a day visit and did not return them as agreed. Nine days later, the mother finally found them in another state.

The appellate court agreed that the visitation order was vague and returned the case for further action by the trial court, but otherwise affirmed the rulings on custody and on the need to impose conditions for supervised visitation. The appellate court also agreed that the father's clinical psychologist could testify about statements made to her, relying on a provision of Missouri law that provided that privileged communications (except those between attorney and client) were not provided legal protections in situations involving child abuse.

After the appellate court rendered its opinion, the father requested a rehearing on the question of permitting his therapist to testify, contending that the evidence in the case did not involve allegations of child abuse. The appellate court disagreed with the father. It acknowledged that the divorce statute did not define child abuse, but stated that the general reporting statute for child abuse applied in such cases. Missouri is one of the states that include emotional abuse in its reporting statute without further defining the term. Abuse is defined as "any physical injury, sexual abuse, or emotional abuse inflicted on a child other than by accidental means by those responsible for the child's care …" § 210.110(1), R.S.Mo. The appellate court found the following with regard to the emotional abuse that the father had inflicted upon the children:

Abuse is defined as "any physical injury, sexual abuse, or emotional abuse inflicted on a child other than by accidental means by those responsible for the child's care …"

> [The lower court's opinion] includes testimony concerning demeaning and unsubstantiated remarks father made to children concerning their mother, as well as evidence concerning father taking the children to another state during a period of visitation and failing to return them as agreed. Theses action and the effect they had on the children were not the result of "accidental means." *A parent who demeans the other parent by inappropriate remarks to children, or who fails to return children to their primary custodian at the*

> *appointed time under the circumstances in evidence in this case, adversely affects the children's welfare. Such conduct can constitute emotional abuse* and is consistent with a decision to appoint a guardian *ad litem* as was done in this case. *Id.* at 632. (Emphasis supplied).

Since the evidence of the father's actions against the mother was sufficient for a finding of abuse or suspected abuse, the appellate court dismissed the request for a rehearing.

Given that empathy is the element most critical to a child's safety and well being, this group of parental behaviors is extremely troubling.

Chapter Fifteen

Operational Definition: Preschool

The clusters of behaviors cited in the previous chapters that are identified with emotional maltreatment cut across the three age groups — preschool, latency, and adolescence. There is one parental behavior, however, that is basically unique to preschool.

> **DEFINITION**
>
> ***The parent does not help the child to learn the basic skills of feeding, bathing, and dressing as well as other skills for independence.***

Parental Behaviors

The child is regularly ignored, rejected, or cursed when he/she asks for assistance. In other words, the parent may exhibit both emotionally abusive and neglectful behaviors toward a small child who needs help. The routines of child care that are usually extended to small children who have not yet learned how to feed themselves, pour a drink of water or milk, get their most basic clothes on or find a warm coat to wear are not performed by the parent. The child is at least left to fend for himself, but may also be subjected to ridicule and shaming when he is unable to care for himself.

This parent may try to assign the care of this child to an older child who may or may not follow through. Leaving the child alone may also be a manifestation of this type of emotional maltreatment for the parent may just leave the child in an apartment or house with the intent that he will take care of himself. In other situations the child is left for long periods, even overnight, with siblings who are not able or willing to care for him.

There may also be a situation when one parent is basically challenging the other parent to take over the care of the child by refusing to see to his needs. The child is a pawn between the two adults in a struggle to determine who has to get up at night, change diapers, or perform other necessary childcare functions.

Implications

Given that empathy is the element most critical to a child's safety and well being, this group of parental behaviors is extremely troubling. In some cases the parent's level of mental functioning could be a reason for a refusal to care for the child, perhaps in a misguided and dangerous attempt to make the child independent. A serious lack of knowledge regarding child development could precipitate this maltreatment if left unaddressed.

A serious lack of knowledge regarding child development could precipitate this maltreatment if left unaddressed.

Other possible reasons for this lack of appropriate care are also alarming. This may be a parent who can't feel or identify with the child, thinks the child is lazy or irresponsible, or believes the child is deliberately not learning self-care as a get-back to the parent. There are triggering possibilities such as drug or alcohol stupor, general laziness, or just not caring.

Regardless of the parent's intent, this child is not only lacking necessary physical care, but is not being encouraged to learn the steps of the process of self-care that come with appropriate parental modeling. His emotional development is also being ignored and neglected.

The case of *In re M.C.,* 917 S.W.2d 268, 39 Tex.Sup.J. 373 (Tex. 1996) demonstrates this type of circumstance. A trial court terminated a mother's rights because of the "extraordinarily unsanitary conditions" in which her children were living. A lower appellate court reversed that judgment, finding no evidence that the mother had "endangered" the children. The Supreme Court of Texas accepted the appeal of this reversal and found that neglect existed to such a level that there was legally sufficient evidence for the termination.

Texas provides for termination of parental rights if the parent "knowingly" allows a child to remain in conditions that endanger the "physical or emotional well-being of the child." The evidence was that the mother had, on more than one occasion, left the children, ages four and under, alone. When they were found wandering on a highway at night, the mother was not concerned. The children were eating off the floor and out of the garbage. There was dirt, garbage, and feces throughout the house. The children wore soiled diapers and clothing. Dead roaches were found in the baby's bottles. Although the children were often ill with diarrhea and vomiting, the mother appeared unconcerned and did not show up for doctor's appointments.

The Court could have focused on the damage being done to the emotional development of the children, but unfortunately, did not.

Based upon this evidence, the Supreme Court of Texas found that, although there was no physical abuse of the children, the evidence of physical neglect was more than adequate to support termination. The Court could have focused on the damage being done to the emotional development of the children, but unfortunately, did not. There is no doubt that the other prong of the test, i.e. whether the "emotional well-being" of the child is endangered, was also easily satisfied in this case.

The issue of the long-term damage inflicted on children by emotional abuse and neglect and the potential impact of that damage on the community as a whole, make it too important a topic to address in any way other than head on.

Chapter Sixteen

Meeting the Challenge

Not all will agree that the clusters of behaviors discussed constitute emotional maltreatment, even when several are combined. Many professionals as well as parents prefer to take the position on emotional maltreatment that many people take on pornography, "I don't know how to define it, but I know it when I see it." This approach hasn't helped our communities deal with obscenity, and it will not help us protect children from emotional maltreatment. The issue of the long-term damage inflicted on children by emotional abuse and neglect and the potential impact of that damage on the community as a whole, make it too important a topic to address in any way other than head on.

We must be proactive, focused, and sensitive to individual and community opinions as we develop a plan of action to heighten the awareness of the community to the problem and, at the same time, provide strategies to bring about needed change. These changes are most likely to occur if each system, e.g. education, day care, child protective services, health, and the judiciary, evaluates its role and responsibility in protecting children from emotional maltreatment. After a system analysis, each section of the community must set goals to ensure the safety of children.

PHASE ONE

A Well-Coordinated Public Awareness Campaign

We must believe that major shifts in community attitudes are possible. We have seen such shifts in a community's stance on smoking and drunk driving. The effort to effect change must begin with public education and public awareness. Since many people obviously do not understand the harm of emotional maltreatment, our efforts to educate will be a challenge. However, considering what was accomplished by MADD in a short period, this is not an unattainable goal. The public wants a reduction in violence and increase in personal safety. Schools want to serve children who are able and ready to learn. Business wants a pool of employees who are emotional healthy and stable. The community wants families who are productive, healthy and sound. Pervasive emotional maltreatment of children is an impediment to all of these community needs. Prevention of emotional abuse and neglect, along with its concomitant purpose of promoting emotional health within a family, would have a positive impact for all.

Prevent Child Abuse America (PCAA), formerly the National Committee to Prevent Child Abuse, an organization based in Chicago that is dedicated to child abuse prevention in all forms, disseminates a public awareness campaign each April for Child Abuse Prevention Month. This campaign was well designed for many years by the Ad Council. The public service announcements sought to educate the public about child abuse and the resulting harm. As a part of the campaign, PCAA did a nationwide survey to determine the level of understanding that people had regarding child abuse. As national publicity and information regarding child abuse increased nationwide, the percentage of respondents who verbalized their disapproval of child abuse increased dramatically. There is no way to answer whether respondents actually changed their opinions and subsequently their behaviors, or whether they answered according to what they knew to be the generally accepted belief or approach. Regardless, raising the public's consciousness about the issue of emotional maltreatment, even if they only give lip service to acknowledging the harm done by such abuse, is a necessary starting place.

An effective public awareness campaign can accomplish several secondary goals that will be of benefit to professionals as well as parents and the community as a whole. These goals include:

1. The dialogue and discussion that naturally occur in planning and implementing such a campaign, as well as the public discussions that follow, will begin the much needed process of establishing and clarifying community standards for the emotional treatment of children. As of now, there has not been such a dialogue, much less a consensus or refining of community standards in this area. The discussion that will emanate from a PR campaign will have tremendous value.
2. This public awareness initiative will also create an uneasiness or discomfort in the community with regard to public displays of emotional maltreatment. When specific behaviors such as shaming, belittling, name calling, ridicule and heinous threats are identified as harmful, people who witness these behaviors, as well as those who might otherwise commit such acts, are sensitized to the stigma and general lack of acceptance by the public. We will have achieved a great deal when someone at the mall is as uncomfortable or concerned when he hears a parent say, "You're just a stupid idiot," as he would be to see the parent slap the child. When that happens, we would have made the first step, an important one, in the process of change. Parents or other caretakers may feel uncomfortable enough to use these tactics only in private, but that is progress. It is certainly more than we have now.
3. The campaign will naturally identify the effects and implications for the community as a whole, since all adults who come in contact with children have been permitted to make comments and exhibit behaviors that can emotionally harm a child. Public awareness will not be directed only toward parents or custodians. It will enlighten the public on how all adults affect the life of a child.
4. Finally, a public awareness campaign will logically highlight and promote prevention as the primary strategy to develop emotionally healthy children. Any thinking parent or professional will want to protect children from this type of maltreatment. As

community standards evolve, conscientious adults will move to prevent the emotional assault on children that has heretofore been virtually ignored. Prevention initiatives have been proven to be the most cost effective interventions in preventing abuse, particularly when done thoughtfully and with the support of the whole community.

For a public awareness campaign such as this to be effective, it would need to be coordinated with various systems and appear under the auspices of education, social services, the medical community and mental health, the courts and the business community.

PHASE TWO

Evaluation and Planning by Individual Systems to Prevent Emotional Maltreatment

The following steps that could occur in each of these sectors are certainly not exhaustive. With more understanding and analysis, professionals in each area will be able to refine and enlarge on these suggestions. However, based on the information we have presented drawn from experience, research, and synthesis, the steps outlined could be a beginning point for discussion.

Day Care and Early Childhood Education

1. Most day care operators, day care staff, and early childhood educators are required to have on-going training in child development, new research or teaching methods. This provides a forum and a logical place to begin. Training on the critical aspects of emotional health along with training on emotional maltreatment are necessary in order to begin to build an understanding in this group. All of these people have a tremendous influence on children. Their training must begin with establishing an understanding that each person in the life of a young child has the potential each day to have a good or a bad emotional interaction with that child. The critical need for empathy to be shown to and encouraged in children is something that

every early childhood worker must internalize as crucial to the well being of the child.

2. Since the nurturance of emotional health in children is critical in the age group birth to five years, early intervention and remediation is extremely important. For this reason, children who access services such as day care, infant stimulation and developmental programs, enrichment programs, Early Headstart, Parents as Teachers, Healthy Families America, and other parent education programs should be evaluated for evidence of emotional damage or delay. The authors are not experts in evaluation and testing; our colleagues in psychometry can offer guidance on methods for evaluating emotional health and the existence of damage from maltreatment. However, the necessary testing instrument must be adequate to provide an analysis based on the statutory standard that would trigger the intervention of CPS and the provision of services and oversight to a family. In many states, that standard is whether there is damage to the psychological capacity or stability of a child that substantially impairs the child's ability to function within a normal range of performance. The need for this type of evaluation could certainly provoke interest in the development of such an instrument, if there is none available.
3. For many parents of children birth to five, day care and other programs that serve children in this age group are natural avenues through which information on emotional health as well as emotional maltreatment could be disseminated. Early childhood programs should be encouraged through their accreditation entities to provide information and training on these subjects to parents.

Schools

1. The school and the family are the only entities common to all children. Therefore, it is essential that the school and the family are closely aligned in their approach to assuring the emotional health of children. The emotional health of children is of

critical importance to the achievement of goals generally set for education, e.g. higher test scores and a school environment conducive to learning. Given that many parents of the children for whom we have the most concern failed at school themselves, it falls to the school to systematically build a bridge to the family. Parents have a responsibility to work with the school, but educators, as the professionals, must be proactive in their efforts to build and sustain a partnership with the family.

We have asked a lot of the education system over the years, resulting in a common lament among teachers, "I just want to teach. I shouldn't have to be the parent also." In reality, the two responsibilities are intimately intertwined in the development of emotional health in the child. Research tells us that the success of the child in school depends on his emotional health. The home and family are the two most significant influences on the child, and their ability to work together is critical.

2. The classroom as a secondary family to the child is a logical place to promote emotional health in children as well as to protect against emotional maltreatment. The interactions of the teacher with each child, as well as the interactions of children with each other, are all opportunities to promote caring, empathy, and understanding of feelings. Teachers must be willing to develop this atmosphere. Therefore, they need training on the elements of emotional health as well as understanding emotional maltreatment and how to cultivate empathy in the classroom.
3. Current research strongly suggests that children need age-appropriate opportunities for success in order to develop emotional health. The school takes on a critical role in making sure that each child experiences accomplishment. Validating the worth of each student could involve a different approach to "success" than we have had in the past, but this is certainly possible, given the broad activities of the school.

These two needs, a sense of family in the classroom and opportunities for success for each child, will develop the "connectedness" to the school that is so necessary for a child to develop normally in all areas. It will enhance the learning process, keep the child in school, reduce violence and be a major step in keeping the school and the child safe.

Child Protective Services

It is not by accident that CPS does not appear first on the list of proposed steps to address emotional maltreatment. For too long we have looked to the CPS system to solve most of the problems regarding child abuse. By doing so, we have severely limited our approach as well as our success in reducing or eliminating child abuse. The responsibility of CPS, along with law enforcement, is to investigate cases of child abuse and ensure the safety of the children. This has been a monumental task given the increasing number of reports.

In the case of emotional maltreatment, and to a large extent all forms of child abuse, the most effective approach involves the efforts of a community to prevent abuse before it happens. The responsibility of CPS, as mandated by statue, is normally not triggered until at least some damage has occurred. CPS is responsible for intervention after the harm. In some areas, CPS has advanced the cause of prevention. However, with their huge responsibility in the investigation and treatment of child abuse, resources are severely stretched to meet minimum standards of their mandate. They do, however, have a major role to play in promoting an awareness of the problem of emotional maltreatment, given their expertise and commitment. Expecting them to solve this problem is unreasonable.

In the case of emotional maltreatment, and to a large extent all forms of child abuse, the most effective approach involves the efforts of a community to prevent abuse before it happens.

Instead, let us determine the contributions that the CPS system can make within their mandated role.

1. It is urgent that the CPS system educates itself on all aspects of emotional maltreatment of children. Since this type of child abuse has not been identified as a priority, training for CPS workers has been limited in this area. CPS must expose its workers to new research on the results of emotional trauma to children. Given the pervasiveness of emotional maltreatment, the staff of all social service agencies should receive training. Ironically, waiting rooms and interview rooms are often the site for extreme emotional maltreatment of children.
2. Based on available research that lack of empathy on the part of a parent or caretaker is the critical variable in assessing risk of abuse, CPS workers and supervisors must include assessment of parental empathy toward the child(ren) as a part of all investigations. An assessment tool needs to be developed to assist workers in analyzing the emotional component of parent-child interactions. Since all investigations normally include critical elements, the element of empathy could be included after appropriate training.
3. After CPS professionals are well trained in emotional maltreatment, agencies should exercise their responsibility and train mandated reporters on the elements of law and policy regarding emotional maltreatment. The serious damage done to children and to society as a whole as a result of emotional abuse and neglect must be emphasized to those community persons identified in the child abuse and neglect laws. Not since the 1970's, when federal law identified mandated reporters, has the CPS system made a major effort to educate reporters. The seriousness of emotional maltreatment justifies this type of effort.
4. With the help of the mental health community, CPS must reevaluate the impact of drug/alcohol addiction and mental illness on the safety and welfare of children. Although it may not be as dramatic as scalding or a fractured skull, the outcome of

emotional maltreatment (particularly neglect) emanating from addiction or mental illness of the caretaker may be just as harmful in the long run. We have developed a strong community standard regarding the damage of sexual abuse although it does not strictly meet the standard of "imminent harm." That approach is appropriate for emotional maltreatment also, given our current knowledge and research on the long-term damage to children by emotional maltreatment. This approach would necessitate the reexamination of the concept of neglect as an extremely serious threat to children.

The Legal System

As the voice of authority in the interpretation and application of the law, judges, and other court officials have a tremendous opportunity to use their influence to effect a major part of the community response to emotional maltreatment of children. Frequently, the court is the principal voice for children. Because of their control over the courtroom, the judiciary is essential for change.

1. Through means such as continuing legal education requirements, law school curricula and the National Council on Juvenile and Family Court Judges, judges must be trained on the newest research and information relating to the emotional maltreatment of children. Resource professionals, as well as staff development personnel for CPS, could assist with this.
2. Attorneys who serve as guardians *ad litem*, as well as volunteer guardians *ad litem* or CASA volunteers, should receive specialized training on the identification and effects of emotional maltreatment. Persons serving in these capacities represent the child's best interests and provide information to the court that is ultimately used in case planning. These people need to be aware of abuse that has no immediate physical manifestations, but that will be devastating to the child, his future family and the community as a whole.

> Emotional abuse and neglect often occur within the context of a divorce proceeding.

3. Emotional abuse and neglect often occur within the context of a divorce proceeding. Typically, no one individual represents the interests of the child in this process. It would be extremely helpful if the court would require that all parties to divorce cases where children are involved seek counseling to ensure that the children are not used as pawns in contested divorces, custody battles, and visitation squabbles. The court could maintain a list of approved counselors from which the parents could choose, or the court system could provide mandatory parenting education sessions around the issue of minimizing the emotional damage to a child while the divorce is in progress.
4. Those in the legal system can take a part in cleaning up confusion with regard to inappropriate or inadequate statutory language covering emotional maltreatment. Lawyers and judges constantly deal with the implementation and interpretation of law. Using their influence to ensure that the definition of harm caused by emotional maltreatment follows model language and that such abuse stands alone and separate from other types of abuse would be of great benefit to those working in the field.

The Medical Community and Mental Health

Parents value input and guidance from health professionals. They quote the doctor with trust and respect. This carries over to the nursing profession and other medical personnel.

These particular professionals have a tremendous amount of influence on parents, which translates into a great deal of responsibility. Parents also seek out mental health counselors or therapists to deal with serious behavioral issues. Their expectations are very high, reflecting the esteem in which so many mental health professionals are held. For this reason the health profession as a whole is needed to promote emotional health in children and identify emotional maltreatment.

1. All health care professionals must be trained in current research on emotional health and emotional maltreatment, including the implications of this research for the general health of the child. Misreading symptoms of emotional abuse or neglect can result in the delay of treatment and remediation or, worse yet, result in no treatment at all since the only professional who sees some children prior to age five is the medical doctor or nurse practitioner.
2. Health professionals, e.g. public health and private practitioners, should take every opportunity to evaluate the child as holistically as possible. There is no doubt that emotional health impacts physical health. A holistic approach would definitely further the goals of ensuring the best possible diagnosis, treatment plan and overall result.
3. Although mental health professionals are a tremendous resource for understanding mental illness, the diagnosis of emotional abuse or neglect is not found in any classification set forth by American Academy of Mental Disorders (AAMD). While emotional maltreatment may not be a diagnosis, it certainly can be the cause of mental health problems. Counselors and therapists must be vigilant and move past the presenting problems to underlying causes that may often be emotional maltreatment.
4. All those in the medical and mental health community should use their voices and influence in the community to promote awareness and understanding of the seriousness of emotional maltreatment of children. Again, these voices will be given credence and respect.

...the diagnosis of emotional abuse or neglect is not found in any classification set forth by American Academy of Mental Disorders (AAMD).

The Community—Business, Civic Leaders, Parents

As professionals are trained on the problem of emotional maltreatment, this knowledge can translate into a community response in all other areas. Sharing and shaping of information by professionals will allow a community to begin the process of integrating this information into their day-to-day care of children. Over time, a consensus or community standard will emerge that will provide the best environment for children to grow and develop into emotionally healthy citizens.

1. Civic leaders and parents will examine and address how children are treated in such activities as organized sports, the arts, scouting, and other activities that can greatly impact them outside the home and school.
2. Business and corporate leaders will utilize their influence to strengthen families by providing support through Employee Assistance Programs, job-site opportunities for parenting education, release time for school conferences, promoting quality day care, and including family support benefits in employee benefit packages.
3. Discussion of emotional health in children and the hurt of emotional maltreatment can be subjects for PTA programs, school conferences, community forums, communities of faith, and programs presented at civic organizations.

The Prevention Community

There is no doubt that the focus of all efforts must be to prevent emotional maltreatment. By the time CPS takes a report, the likelihood that serious damage has been done to a child is high. Repairing harm is a difficult task. Providing support to families so that harm does not occur in the first place must be the aim of every section within a community.

There is no doubt that the focus of all efforts must be to prevent emotional maltreatment.

Since the 1970's, the child abuse prevention movement has been instrumental in marshalling community efforts to prevent abuse before it occurs as well as to prevent re-victimization. In the beginning, these efforts were tentative and scattered, but never lacking in zeal and commitment. In the last ten years, prevention programs have redefined themselves and their efforts to focus on strengthening families instead of merely advocating to stop abuse. By moving to a strength-based approach, the prevention community has broadened its impact and enhanced the viability of programming.

In the last ten years, prevention programs have redefined themselves and their efforts to focus on strengthening families instead of merely advocating to stop abuse.

As a result of this change, the prevention community is now in a position to teach, guide, and nurture new parents toward providing an emotionally healthy environment for children. In order to do this, however, professionals, volunteers, and paraprofessionals must set goals that would include:

1. All persons working in the prevention community must be trained in the causes, definitions, and impact of emotional maltreatment.
2. Material that is sensitive to current knowledge and research on emotional health and emotional maltreatment would be integrated into all programs, especially those designed for parents such as Healthy Parents, Parents as Teachers, Success by Six, Healthy Start, Even Start, Early Headstart, the Exchange Club volunteer parent aides and Parents Anonymous.
3. The advocacy efforts of the prevention community need to lobby for any necessary changes in law or policy that would protect children from emotional maltreatment. Legislators in states where emotional abuse is not included in the reporting statutes

or is inappropriately defined need to be asked to initiate legislation that conforms to the model language.

Perhaps the most important role prevention can play is that of community organizer, collaborator, and bridge builder. This has been the historic role of prevention—to "give the work away" to other systems and organizations, always seeking to integrate prevention efforts into the programs and efforts of others and institutionalize them wherever possible. Prevention can be a catalyst for change, drawing attention to the benefits that all systems in the community will derive from prevention efforts.

The Future

With a proactive approach to emotional maltreatment, in ten years we could expect a major shift in community attitudes regarding the care and value of children. It would be just as shocking and reprehensible to see adults deride, ridicule, and shame children in public as it would be to see an adult take a bat to or slap a child. Coaches would use emotionally appropriate means to motivate children; the parents in the grandstand would be encouraging and positive to all children. Teachers would be excited to know that the secret to success in school is the face and demeanor of the person standing in the front of the class. They would be encouraged to determine why a child is withdrawn or sad. Judges would look past what parents say in the courtroom when children are standing before the bench in dependency and delinquency cases. The question in the minds of all professions who touch the lives of troubled children would be, "Why?"

It would be just as shocking and reprehensible to see adults deride, ridicule, and shame children in public as it would be to see an adult take a bat to or slap a child.

Finally, words, attitudes, and influence will be seen as opportunities to love and never as weapons that will cause harm. Our society can and must protect our young, seizing every opportunity to teach, encourage and love. This love must be extended not only to those children who are sweet and obedient, but to those who are often difficult to love, those who tax our patience and push us to the limit of endurance. Even as we intervene to change behaviors with discipline and limits, we do so with a sense of concern and a question, "Why?"

Every child who plays in the yard, sits in a classroom, chases a baseball, swings in the park, goes to daycare or asks our help represents a future family. In the early years of a child's life, each of us has a time-limited opportunity to make an impact that can change not only the child's future, but our own. It all begins with recognizing the tremendous potential for each interaction, each word, each gesture that we have with a child. This opportunity continues with looking past surface behaviors such as giving up, detachment, aggression, or sadness and asking ourselves, "Why?" Why is this child quietly standing on the fringes of the group? Why is this child tormenting anyone he sees as weak? Why does this child lack joy? Why is this child immobilized and unable to move forward? We must first learn all of the questions that need to be asked, and then diligently seek the answers.

In the early years of a child's life, each of us has a time-limited opportunity to make an impact that can change not only the child's future, but our own.

• • • • • •

As we have seen in the past, we are capable of confronting and solving complex problems that threaten our children. Not only will emotional maltreatment prevention require that we examine our personal attitudes and behaviors, we will be required to look at children with our eyes and with our hearts.

The lives of all children, not just those who are maltreated, depend on our search for the answer to "Why?"

BIBLIOGRAPHY

Baily, T.F. and Baily, W.H. (1986). *Operational Definitions of Child Emotional Maltreatment*. Final Report. Washington, D.C.: National Center of Child Abuse and Neglect.

Barnet, A.B. and Barnet, R.J. (1998). *The Youngest Minds*. New York: Simon & Schuster.

Blum, R.W., Beuhring, T. and Rinehart, P.M. (2000). *Protecting Teens: Beyond Race, Income and Family Structure*. Minneapolis, MN: Center for Adolescent Health.

Brazelton, T. B. and Greenspan, S. I. (2000). *The Irreducible Needs of Children*. Cambridge, Massachusetts: Perseus Publishing.

Garbarino, J. (1999). *Lost Boys: Why Our Sons Turn Violent and How We Can Save Them.* New York: Anchor Books.

Garbarino, J. and Garbarino, A. (1994, rev'd 2nd Ed.). *Emotional Maltreatment of Children*. Chicago: Prevent Child Abuse America.

Goleman, D., (1995). *Emotional Intelligence.* New York: Bantam Books.

Goleman, D., (1998). *Working with Emotional Intelligence*. New York: Bantam Books.

Karr-Morse, R. and Wiley, M.S. (1997). *Ghosts from the Nursery: Tracing the Roots of Violence*. New York: Atlantic Monthly Press.

Kessler, D.B. and Dawson, P. (Eds.) (1999). *Failure to Thrive and Pediatric Undernutrition*. Baltimore: Paul H. Brookes Publishing.

Kindlon, D. and Thompson, M. (1999). *Raising Cain,* New York: Ballentine Books.

Klein, J.D. (1997). *The National Longitudinal Study on Adolescent Health: Preliminary Results: Great Expectations.* JAMA, 278 (10), 864-865.

Korfmacher, J. (1998). *Emotional Neglect: Being Hurt by What Is Not There.* Chicago: Prevent Child Abuse America.

Kvols, K.J.(1998). *Redirecting Children's Behavior.* Seattle: Parenting Press.

McNeely, C.A., Nonnemaker, J.M. & Blum, R.W. (2002). "Promoting School Connectedness: Evidence from the National Longitudinal Study of Adolescent Health." *Journal of School Health,* 72 (4) 138-146.

Meyers, J. E.B. (1998). *Legal Issues in Child Abuse and Neglect Practice.* Thousand Oaks: SAGE Publications.

Monteleone, J.A. (1996). *Recognition of Child Abuse for the Mandated Reporter.* St. Louis: G.W. Medical Publishing, Inc.

Monteleone, J.A. (1998). *A Parent & Teacher's Handbook on Identifying and Preventing Child Abuse.* St. Louis: G.W. Medical Publishing, Inc.

National Center for Child Abuse and Neglect (2001). "Understanding the Effects of Maltreatment on Early Brain Development" [online]. Retrieved from http://www.calib.com/nccanch/pubs/focus/earlybrain.cfm.

O'Hagen, K. (1993). *Emotional and Psychological Abuse of Children.* Toronto: University of Toronto Press.

Ounce of Prevention Fund. (1996). *Starting Smart: How Early Experiences Affect Brain Development.* Chicago: Ounce of Prevention Fund.

Perry, B.D. (1998a). "Biologic Relativity: Time and the Developing Child" [online]. Retrieved from http://www.childtrauma.org/biolo_relativity.htm

Perry, B.D. & Pollard, R. (1998b). "Homeostasis, Stress, Trauma and Adaptation: A Neurodevelopmental View of Childhood Trauma" [online]. Retrieved from http://www.childtrauma.org/pollard.htm

Perry, B.D. (1999). "Memories of Fear: How the Brain Stores and Retrieves Physiologic States, Feelings, Behaviors and Thoughts from Traumatic Events" [online]. Retrieved from http://www.childtrauma.org/Memories.htm

Perry, B.D. (2000a). "Traumatized Children: How Childhood Trauma Influences Brain Development" [online]. Retrieved from http://www.childtrauma.org/trau_CAMI.htm

Perry, B.D. (2000b). "Brain Structure and Function II: Special Topics Informing Work with Maltreated Children" [online]. Retrieved from http://www.childtrauma.org/brain_II.htm

Perry, B.D. (2001). "Violence and Childhood: How Persisting Fear Can Alter the Developing Child's Brain" [online]. Retrieved from http://www.childtrauma.org/Vio_child.htm

Resnick, M.D., Bearman, P.S., Blum, R.W., et al. (1997). *Protecting Adolescents from Harm: Findings from the National Longitudinal Study on Adolescent Health.* JAMA, 278 (10), 823-832.

Rosenstein, P. (1995). *Parental Levels of Empathy as Related to Risk Assessment in Child Protective Services.* Child Abuse & Neglect, 19 (11), 1349-1360.

Sedlack, A.J. & Broadhurst, D.B. (1996). *Executive Summary of the Third National Incidence Study of Child Abuse and Neglect.* Washington, D.C.: U.S. Department of Health and Human Services.

Shapiro, L.E. (1997). *How to Raise a Child with a High EQ.* New York: HarperCollins Publishers.

Stern, D. (1987). *The Interpersonal World of the Infant.* New York: Basic Books.

U.S. Advisory Board on Child Abuse and Neglect. (1991). *Creating Caring Communities: Blueprint for an Effective Federal Policy on Child Abuse and Neglect.* Washington, D.C.: Government Printing Office.

U.S. Department of Health and Human Services. (1993). *A Report to Congress: The National Center on Child Abuse and Neglect Study of High Risk Child Abuse and Neglect Groups.* Washington, D.C.: National Clearinghouse on Child Abuse and Neglect Information.

U.S. Department of Health and Human Services. (2001). *Child Maltreatment, 1999.* Washington, D.C.: Government Printing Office.

U.S. Department of Health and Human Services. (1999). *Mental Health: A Report of the Surgeon General—Executive Summary.* Rockville, MD: U.S. Department of Health and Human and Human Services.

• • • Cases Cited • • •

Cynthia C. v. Superior Court, 72 Cal.App.4th 1196, 85 Cal.Rptr.2d 669 (Cal.App.4th Dist. 1999)

Department of Health & Welfare v. Doe (In re Doe), 133 Idaho 826, 992 P.2d 1226 (Idaho Ct. App. 1999)

Director of the Dallas County Child Protective Services Unit of the Texas Department of Human Services v. Bowling, 833 S.W.2d 730 (Tex. App. Dallas 1992)

Doe v. Doe (In re Doe), 133 Idaho 805, 992 P.2d 1205 (Idaho 1999)

E.J.R. v. Young (In re J.R.), 162 Vt. 219, 646 A.2d 1284 (1994)

In Interest of C.N.T., 771 P.2d 561, 1989 Kan.App. LEXIS 159 (Kan.Ct.App. 1989)

In Interest of E.B.L. 501 N.W.2d 547 (Iowa 1993)

In Interest of N.H., 383 N.W.2d 570 (Iowa 1986)

In re Bedwell, 160 Mich.App. 168, 408 N.W.2d 65 (1987)

In re C.A.R., 214 Mont. 174, 693 P.2d 1214 (Mont. 1984)

In re: Carrie B, 1990 Conn. Super.LEXIS 155 (Conn. Super. Ct. July 23, 1990)

In re Edward C., 126 Cal.App.3d 193, 178 Cal.Rptr. 694 (Cal. App. 1st Dist. 1981)

In re Gentry, 142 Mich.App. 701, 369 N.W.2d 889 (Mich.App. 1985)

In re Heather A., 52 Cal.App.4th 183, 60 Cal.Rptr.2d 315 (Cal. App. 2d Dist. 1996)

In re: Jessica T., 1993 Conn.Super. LEXIS 3480 (Conn. Super. Ct. Dec. 20, 1993)

In re: Kathleen R., 1993 Conn.Super. LEXIS 2537 (Conn. Super. Ct., June 14, 1993)

In re M.C., 917 S.W.2d 268, 39 Tex.Sup.J. 373 (Tex. 1996)

In re M.W., 1998 Minn.App. LEXIS 1167 (Minn. Ct. App. Oct. 20, 1998)

In re: Orwell, 1993 Ohio App. LEXIS 6180 (Ohio Ct. App. Montgomery County, 1993)

In re S.L., 419 N.W.2d 689 (S.D. 1988)

In re Shelley J., 68 Cal.App.4th 322, 79 Cal.Rptr.2d 922 (Cal.App.6th Dist. 1998)

In the Interest of Ra.R., 793 P.2d 767 (Kan. Ct. App. 1990)

In the Matter of A.M., 304 Mont. 379, 22 P.3d 185 (2001)

In Interest of N.N., 278 N.W.2d 150 (N.D. 1979)

Interest of Cheatwood, 108 Idaho 218, 697 P.2d 1232 (Idaho Ct. App. 1985)

Interest of D., 253 N.W.2d 870 (N.D. 1977)

J.T. v. Arkansas Dep't. of Human Serv., 329 Ark. 243, 947 S.W.2d 761 (Ark. 1997)

Jackson v. W., 14 Va.App. 391, 419 S.E.2d 385 (1992)

Matter of Shane T., 453 N.Y.S.2d 590 (N.Y. Fam. Ct. 1982)

Navarrette v. Texas Dep't. of Human Resources, 669 S.W.2d 849 (Tex.App. El Paso 1984)

Parker v. Department of Pensions and Sec., 437 So.2d 551 (Ala. Civ. App. 1983)

People v. D.A.K., 198 Colo. 11, 596 P.2d 747 (1979); appeal dismissed, 444 U.S. 987, 100 S.Ct. 515, 62 L.Ed.2d 416 (1979)

Pilger v. Pilger, 972 S.W.2d 628 (Mo.Ct.App. 1998)

Roark v. Roark, 551 N.E.2d 865 (Ind. Ct. App. 1990)

Santosky v. Kramer, 455 U.S. 745, 102 S.Ct. 1388, 71 L.Ed.2d (1982)

State v. Eventyr J., 120 N.M. 463, 902 P.2d 1066 (Ct.App. 1995)

State v. Stevens, 797 P.2d 1133 (Utah Ct. App. 1990)

State ex rel. C.J.K., 774 So. 2d 107 (La. 2000)

State ex rel. J.L.V. v. State, 958 P.2d 943 (Utah Ct. App. 1998)

State in Interest of Four Minor Children v. D.W., 585 So.2d 1222 (La.Ct.App. 2 Cir. 1991)

State in Interest of Quilter, 424 So.2d 394 (La.Ct.App. 2 Cir. 1982)

Stone v. Daviess County Div. Child Servs., 656 N.E.2d 824 (Ind. Ct. App. 1995)

Stuart v. Tarrant County Child Welfare Unit, 677 S.W.2d 273 (Tex.. App. Fort Worth 1984)

Texas Dep't. of Human Services v. Boyd, 727 S.W.2d, 531, 30 Tex.Sup.Ct.J. 352 (Tex. 1987)

Wisconsin v. Yoder, 406 U.S. 205 (233-34), 92 S. Ct. 1526, 1542, 32 L.Ed.2d 15 (1971)

Red Clay & Vinegar

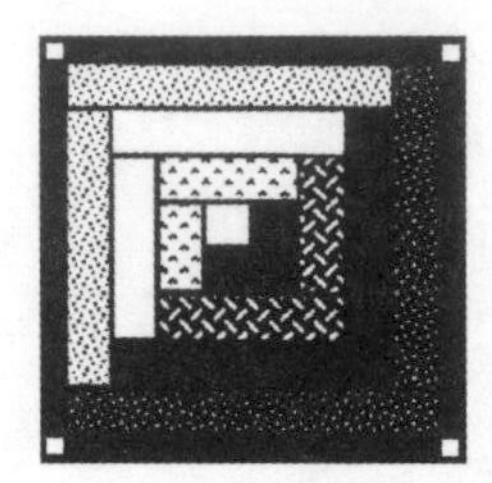

Over the years, Southerners have used various "home remedies" to treat ailments, injuries, and diseases. Passed down through generations, these folk medicines usually relied on ingredients found locally, such as herbs, plants, and minerals. The soil in parts of Alabama, Mississippi, and Georgia is a distinctive red clay, and this red clay is one ingredient often found in these remedies.

Vinegar, a common household product used for making pickles and mopping the floor, is also used in many Southern elixirs, compresses, and poultices.

All families are a mixture of strengths and weaknesses, and red clay and vinegar are symbolic of a family's ability to find effective ways to heal themselves, building on their strengths and seeking practical ways to minimize their weaknesses.